About the Author

Christine Jones was born in Coalville, a small coal-mining community in Leicestershire, the heart of the British midlands. She was married in 1970 to Alan and moved to Australia in 1973, with her husband and their two children Andrea and Mark, both under three years, four suitcases and five hundred dollars.

Now happily retired and doting on their six grandchildren. Lockdown boredom pushed her back into writing.

Among the Coal Dust

Christine Jones

Among the Coal Dust

Olympia Publishers
London

www.olympiapublishers.com
OLYMPIA PAPERBACK EDITION

Copyright © Christine Jones 2022

The right of Christine Jones to be identified as author of this work has been asserted in accordance with sections 77 and 78 of the Copyright, Designs and Patents Act 1988.

All Rights Reserved

No reproduction, copy or transmission of this publication may be made without written permission. No paragraph of this publication may be reproduced, copied or transmitted save with the written permission of the publisher, or in accordance with the provisions of the Copyright Act 1956 (as amended).

Any person who commits any unauthorised act in relation to this publication may be liable to criminal prosecution and civil claims for damage.

A CIP catalogue record for this title is available from the British Library.

ISBN: 978-1-80074-726-5

This is a work of creative nonfiction. The events are portrayed to the best of the author's memory. While all the stories in this book are true, some names and identifying details have been changed to protect the privacy of the people involved.

First Published in 2022

Olympia Publishers
Tallis House
2 Tallis Street
London
EC4Y 0AB
Printed in Great Britain

Dedication

Dedicated to the memory of Desmond Isaac Murby and Michael Desmond Murby. During our time on Earth, a life can touch just a few people. Sometimes it can touch many. Desmond and Michael were men who did not receive great recognition in their lives, but were nevertheless great men, and their family thank God every day for the blessing of their lives. To all the Murbys, past and present, know where you came from, be proud of who you are, always follow your heart.

Acknowledgements

To my dad, who told me I could do anything as long as I set my mind to it. To my husband, for all his tireless researching. To my children, Andrea and Mark, for their love and support. And family members for snippets of information, and photos. Paul Williams for allowing me to add his great-grandfather's song and dance routine. Sam Benton and the Thursday writers' group, for their support and encouragement.

CHAPTER ONE
The Man Within the Compass

It was a cold and frosty November evening. Dark clouds had lingered overhead for most of the day. A storm had been predicted by Zachariah Parker, local publican of 'The Man Within the Compass', who thought himself an authority on potential storms due to an old injury in his forefinger which he insists throbs when a storm is brewing.

But the storm as yet had not eventuated. However, the English weather was so unpredictable. Who knew what might happen? If it did happen, Zac would again announce, 'I told you so.'

1910 had so far been a particularly cold year. Another cold, hard winter had been forecast. It seemed winter had arrived earlier than expected.

Zac unlocked the heavy front door of the pub, as he did every evening, then threw another log onto the open fire.

"I think we will need the extra heat tonight, Mother," he said. Zac had taken to calling his wife 'Mother', a term of endearment.

Taking up the hearth brush and dustpan, he proceeded to sweep the old ashes that had fallen from the log before. Just then the front door burst open.

"Ay-up, Zac, looks like a storm brewing."

"Evening, Tommy. What'll it be then?" Zac asked.

"I'll have a pint, ta." Tommy was the first of many to arrive at the local pub tonight. It was a ritual, the same faces most nights, some for a quick pint, others there till closing.

Tommy was always one of the first to arrive, but that night he must have sprinted the full two miles from his home to the pub. "Thirsty tonight are ya, lad? Or ya runnin from the missus?" Zac laughed.

Tommy was a well-liked man of slight stature, carrying a full head of curly brown hair. And although he was in his fifties, he didn't have one grey hair in sight. He was a miner, and had been since he was fourteen years old, just as his father was before him. You could tell the miners, they were the ones who had black around their nails, and in the creases of their hands. Another tell-tale sign were little blue marks on their faces or arms. This was when they had a small cut while below ground and, unable to return to the surface, they would rub coal dust into the cut to stop the bleeding; after a while, it turned blue. There was always an unspoken law between the miners, Zac had said it was like the army. Wherever there is a band of men, bound together for a common cause, you will always find extraordinary friendship and loyalty.

"It's a bit nippy tonight, definitely brass-monkey weather." Tommy continued, "How's that lovely wife of yours?"

"Ah, Sarah's all right thanks, Tommy." Zac replied, handing him a pint with one hand, and wiping the bar top with the other. Leaning closer to Tommy, he quietly asked, "Do you have any tips for the gee gees tomorrow?"

"Well now, let me see." Tommy scratched his brow.

Zac continued, "I heard '*Young Rascal*' will be hard to beat and is a definite contender."

Tommy screwed his face and moved his head from side to side. "Could be worth a couple of bob," he said, but he wasn't convincing.

Zac, who was very keen on horse racing wrote it down.

"Ya know, Tommy, I won five quid t'other day, but not a word to the missus. She'd have me hide."

Just then, Billy Blunder, another regular of the pub, seemed to fly through the door. He was usually the first in, and last out. Billy went straight to the open fire holding his hands over the flames, then rubbing them together.

"Burrrrrr… it's a bloody cold 'un tonight lads, bloody cold enough ta snow."

Billy was an ex-boxer, amateur status. In his day he was handy with his fists, some would say he was nothing more than a street fighter. But these days all he seemed to do was drink, get drunk, and blunder around. After a few pints he was hardly audible. And so, to everyone in the village, he was known as Billy Blunder.

He didn't seem to mind, he knew, or at least he hoped, it was not malicious.

He always said, 'While they are talking about me they are leaving someone else alone.'

Billy's boxing days had left him a little slow on the uptake, but for the most part he was harmless. His wife of twenty years had passed away two years earlier.

Having never been blessed with children, Billy had no family to turn to. Consequently, it took him a long time to come to terms with the loss and being alone.

He had aged a lot over the last two years, his scalp seemed to have grown through his hair, and he had put on a little pudding around the middle. Billy enjoyed his nightly pint, or two, and would always sing on his way home. He would stagger down Cademan Street to the shouts of, 'Shut up!' and, 'Go home Billy, you bloody fool!' He just sang louder. And more often than not, ended up asleep in someone's front garden.

Within half an hour, 'The Man Within the Compass' was packed. Empty glasses passed over headed to the bar, and full ones were passed back. Cigarette smoke filled the room, and the fire crackled. There was so much noise, that everyone had to shout to be heard. These were the nights Zac loved, everyone enjoying themselves, and spending their hard-earned cash.

Danny Price was the local Tailor. His father, George, had taught him everything he knew, and the importance of a well-tailored suit. "A man has the right to be well-suited no matter how much, or how little, money he has to spend," George would say.

Since George's passing ten years earlier, Danny had taken over the shop in town and continued just as his father had taught him.

No one knew exactly how to take Danny. He frequented the pub once a week, every Friday night, and tonight was no exception. A small thin man, very quiet, so quiet that he was rarely heard to utter a word. Some said his father beat all conversation out of him, when he was growing up. George had been quick tempered with Danny and his mother. Probably why he never married.

Danny was a source of dread for Sarah, he often made her stomach turn. She preferred her husband to serve him, and mostly he did, but occasionally she had no choice.

Danny always sat in the same place. Right under the window. Everyone knew that was Danny's Friday chair. It was always vacant when he arrived. If a stranger happened to call in for a quick pint, they would be told, 'That's Danny's chair.' Danny never ordered anything as he came through the door like everyone else. He just sat down and placed his money on the table in front of him.

"Ay-up, Danny," Zac said.

Danny just nodded and continued searching his pockets. Slipping his hand into his breast pocket, he took out a small packet, containing a tiny pair of scissors, and a needle and thread. Squinting, he would thread the needle, tie a knot in the end of the thread, and proceed to sew his lips together, just a couple of stitches, he then put the needle away, and placed the scissors on the table next to his money. Everyone was so used to Danny and paid him no heed.

Staring into space, he would quietly wait. Sarah or Zac would bring him half a pint of beer, and fresh bread and cheese, and take the money from the table.

Then Danny picked up the scissor, cut the stitching in his lips and carried on like nothing had happened. He drank his beer, ate the bread and cheese. Still not saying one word. This was an occurrence that happened every week without fail.

"He ain't all there," Sarah said to Zac. "I wish he'd go somewhere else for his beer and cheese," she continued. But they were used to him, as were the rest of the regulars.

"He's all right, Mother, we all have funny little ways," Zac reassured her. "How about gettin some bread and cheese for Charlie over there, he been waiting a while now," Zac said, nodding in Charlie's direction.

"There's too many funny buggers round these parts, and we seem to get the ruddy lot," Sarah replied.

Just as she was putting old Charlie's homemade bread and cheese in front of him, the pub door flung open, smashing into the wall with a loud thunderous bang. The whole pub went silent and stared toward the door. Alfred Williams entered the pub, hands in the air.

"Bugger! Sorry lads, the wind took it."

"Bloody hell, Alf, thought you were coming through the bloody wall!" Zac said.

Alf was another a regular at the Compass inn. He was a funny old character, who was well liked. He wore his trademark black bowler hat and carried his fine walking stick with an ebony handle. He looked like he just stepped out of the music hall.

Jumping up on the closest table, he proceeded to sing his favourite song, 'Cast Iron Chicken':

How that loveable bird could sing,
It started humming the camels are coming,
And tried to do the highland fling.
Gor blimey!

He proceeded to tap his feet to the highland fling on the tabletop, followed by a high jump, legs stretched so wide he touched his toes with his hands before landing on the wooden floorboards. Looking dapper, he continued dancing. Tipping his bowler hat, then passed it in front of all the onlookers. His performance would get a few pennies, and definitely a mug of ale from Zac.

"One day, mark my words," Sarah said, "One of these days he's gonna fall off that bloody table, what then, eh?"

"Somebody will catch him," Zac said clapping along with everyone else.

"Don't say I didn't warn ya, ya old fool!" Sarah cautioned, heading back to the kitchen.

That night turned out to be much busier than other nights. No reason for it really, you just had days like that, exhausting days. And even more exhausting nights. But that was the life of a publican.

Zachariah Parker had married Sarah Wesley, in 1898 at the Whitwick parish church; during the next ten years they welcomed five surviving children, Ada, Ivy, Zechariah Jr, Sarah, and Herbert. Sadly, in 1899, Sarah's first-born, a daughter, Mary Ann, died after only a few minutes on this earth.

A son, William, was born in October 1906 but he died in January 1907, living only a few months. The doctor could not tell them why, just that unfortunately it happens.

They had been landlord and landlady of 'The Man Within the Compass' for quite some time, moving there in 1908. No one seemed to know where the name came from, but most thought it was a religious thing, maybe masonic. Later it would become known as 'The Rag and Mop', a nickname that stuck until present day.

Situated at the top of Cadman Street, on Loughborough Road, it was not a large establishment. The kitchen was the largest room. This was where the family lived, and prepared food for themselves and the pub. Sarah cooked on a black led open fire cooker, consisting of a small oven with a heavy metal door and two pull-out draws at the bottom. The open fire in the centre needed to be kept at a high temperature to ensure even baking and browning. Sarah would re-black the led every month, the one job she hated.

A large, heavy, well-scrubbed wooden table sat in front of the black led.

Room for all the children to eat at, as well as food preparation and pastry rolling.

They were a well-known, and respected couple within the village of Whitwick, a relatively small community compared to the nearby town of Coalville and the larger city of Leicester. Whitwick was nevertheless a bustling country village. The main industry in the area was coal mining. Every second man was a miner or had something to do with the mines in the area. Every house burnt coal for warmth. The smell from smoke, and dust from the coal, was ever present in the air. Housewives complained that the washing was dirtier when it was brought in from the washline than when it was put out, and it always had a strong smell of coal fires.

But for Zac and Sarah, their piece of heaven was their little pub on the Loughbough road. Albeit hard labour at times, coupled with long hours, they were happy.

They were raising their daughters with the expectation they would become confident young ladies. While their sons would hopefully grow to be responsible, and respected young men.

"Time, gentlemen please!" shouted Zac as he put a scruffy cloth over the beer taps. "Come on, lads, 'ome to ya beds you go."

Zac could be an intimidating person at closing time. A tall, lanky man over six feet, who hardly looked strong enough to pull a pint, but he could lift a barrel of beer by himself with ease. Zac's dark hair had started to show whispers of silver flashes, his sideburns, already silver, looked rather distinguished. He towered over most, which is probably why he intimidated, but he was a kind, and fair man who would stand for no nonsense. Sarah on the other hand, liked her husband to be in charge. She wasn't treated badly by any means. They complimented each other. Their marriage had plenty of love, and respect.

Sally had control of the household, all the children's needs, and the food for the pub, while Zac took care of everything else. Her sweet face was small and round. With deep blue eyes, and brown wavy hair. She was an unassuming person, highly religious, and always humble. Unless you messed with her family, then she could be a wild lioness.

Zac saw the last of the men off the premises and on their way home.

Locking the front door to the pub, he glanced around and said, "Well, Mother, looks like a late night for us, with all this bloody mess to clean up."

Sarah agreed, she started collecting glasses. "Better get on with it then," she said.

Two hours later she slipped into bed, completely exhausted, but glad to be off her feet. She let out a large sigh and closed her eyes just as the first clap of thunder sounded, it was followed very quickly by a flash of lightening.

"Told ya there was gonna be a storm, didn't I?" Zac said triumphantly.

"That's all I need," she said, burying her head under the blanket.

CHAPTER TWO
Loss and School

The next few days, there was a void in the pub. The absence of Billy Blunder. No one had seen him, and he hadn't been to work either. His buddies assumed he must have had a bad case of the flu.

This was the third night in a row that he was a no-show at the Compass inn.

"I am a bit concerned about Billy," Zac said to Tommy. "I was so sure he would be here tonight."

Tommy agreed. "I think I will finish this pint, Zac, and pop down to see if he's all right. How was the old bugger last time ya saw him?"

"He was fine and dandy, he left 'ere singing as usual," Zac said with a concerned look.

Tommy drank down the remainder of his beer, and let out a sigh of contentment, followed by a burp. Placing his glass on the bar. "I'll be off then, Zac, won't be long."

"All right, lad, tell him to get well soon, there's a pint waiting for 'im."

Tommy had a bounce in his step as he made his way down the hill to Billy's house. He passed the Smith brothers, Joe and Henry on his way. "Ay-up, boys, rum weather, you ain't laid eyes on old Billy Blunder have ya?"

"No Tommy, heard he was sick with the flu." Henry said.

Turning into Billy's garden gate, Tommy noticed that the milk was still on the door step. Three bottles, and Billy only had one bottle a day delivered.

Tommy Banged on the door, he was shouting. "Billy! Billy! Are you there? Billy, come on, man, open the door!"

Nothing, no sound at all. It crossed Tommy's mind that he may have gone off to visit his wife's sister, Mable, in Yarmouth. But Billy always said she was a nosey old cow, and he couldn't stand her. No, he had to be inside. Tommy rushed around to the back of the house, once again calling out for Billy to answer the door, he banged on the window, the door and the wall. He could not raise him.

Tommy kicked in the back door. Immediately his hand went to his face, the room smelled like a dead horse. He made his way through Billy's untidy sitting room to the even more filthy kitchen, all the time calling his name.

Making his way up the stairs, Tommy pushed open the door to Billy's bedroom, which was so dark due to the closed heavy black drapes.

Tommy went to the window, and threw back the curtains and opened a window, hoping to reduce the smell a little.

Turning back to the room, he got the shock of his life, Billy was laying on his bed, still fully clothed. Reaching out he touched Billy's hand and pulled away sharply. Billy was so cold, like he had turned to stone. There was a picture of his wife by his side, and an empty pill bottle on the floor. Tommy fell against the wall.

"Oh no. Billy, Billy. Oh no." Tommy could feel his heart beating so fast, it felt like it was trying to escape through his chest.

Running down the stairs and out into the night air. He

called for help.

Running through the wooden front garden gate was Billy's next door neighbour Fred Bassett, he had heard the commotion and rushed to help.

"Get the doctor, I think Billy's dead." Tommy shouted

Fred didn't wait for any explanation; he was on his old rickety bicycle and peddling away.

Dr Wakefield arrived in his little, black, two-man, horse drawn carriage, Billy could not be moved until the Doctor had officially pronounced him deceased. Fred Bassett was then sent to get Mr Dean from Dean & Son undertakers.

By this time there was quite a gathering of neighbours outside at Billy's house, some in disbelief, and others being purely nosey.

The undertakers arrived, Billy's body was gently loaded onto the horse-drawn dray, which had a large wooden box covering the entire rear of the dray.

Tommy returned to the 'Compass Inn' to inform Zac and everyone still at the pub of the fate that had befallen Billy.

"Sit ya self down, lad" Zac said to Tommy. "Sarah, bring Tommy a pint quickly." Tommy was white, and still in shock, as he relayed the events of the last two hours.

Zac called, "Time, gentlemen!" and closed the pub early. Tommy stayed on till way past normal closing time before returning to his home. After checking Tommy would be all right, Zac saw him off the premises and locked up for the night.

Because Billy had no relatives, as far as anyone knew, he was given a basic burial, paid for by all his friends at 'The Man Within the Compass'. He was laid to rest in the Cemetery on Church Lane, where most locals were also laid to rest.

Sarah woke the kids and told them to get dressed for school.

"Ivy! Have you combed ya bloody hair?"

"No, Ma, the brush won't go through, it gets stuck."

"Not again, come 'ere. Ya bloody hair is so curly I swear, I will shave it all off if you don't wear your bed cap." Sarah sighed. "You always look like you've been dragged through an edge backwards."

"Ouch, stop, Ma, it hurts."

A blood curdling scream came from upstairs. It was Ada.

"For cryin' out loud, Ada, that was loud enough to wake the dead. What's up wi' ya?" Sarah said, out of breath from rushing up the stairs. Ada was standing on the bed she shared with both her sisters.

"A creepy crawly thing ran over me foot," Ada squealed. "It's a cockroach, no wait, there's another one." She was jumping on the bed now with her hands covering her eyes. "Ma, there could be more, I hate 'em!"

Ada was still jumping up and down on the bed when one of the small thin wooden legs snapped, sending both her and the bed crashing to the floor with a bang.

Sarah, now furious, had to shout to be heard. "SHUT IT YA BLOODY BABY, NOW LOOK AT WHAT YA DONE!" She was so mad she grabbed Ada and slapped her face. This just made Ada cry much louder than when she squealed.

Zac came storming into the room. "What the hell is goin on? I can hear ya in the back yard. Sounds like ya bein' killed."

Ada tried to explain through her tears about the cockroaches, waving her arms around, "They were this big, Dad!"

"Stop! Stop!" Zac said, "Don't get ya knickers in a twist, it's only a bug, it won't bloody kill ya. Who's gonna fix this bed? That's what I wanna to know."

"Me face hurts as well, cos ma hit me." Ada complained.

"Well, young 'un, you'll have worse than that afore ya die. And if ya don't shut it you'll get something to really make ya cry!" Zac's face was red. He was serious, Ada knew her Dad was mad with her, so she went as quietly as she could.

"Just bugger off to school. Now! Get ya shoes on or you'll be late."

Ivy and Ada had been complaining lately that they didn't want to go to school anymore, crying all the way, insisting they hated school. Sarah had brushed off their whining, telling Zac, 'All kids hate school. Just as we did when we were young.'

Zac wasn't sure this was the case, but he never questioned Sarah dealing with the kids, she knew best, this was her department.

That was until Ivy arrived home an hour late from school. When she got home, she was limping and crying. She told her mother that the headmaster, Mr Bastard, had thrashed her for no reason, and she felt sick. Mr Bastard had been Headmaster of the small school for a few years. He was a lanky, skinny man, with a booming voice, that scared the children so much that they ran in all directions whenever he was near. He had a large, waxed moustache, so stiff surely his wife was stabbed in the face every time he kissed her goodbye. His balding head emphasised his large ears which stuck out so far the children called him elephant head.

Sarah checked Ivy's bruises, then warmed up some milk and sent her to her bed to settle down. She told Zac that Ivy nor Ada would be going to school until that headmaster got off his high horse and apologised.

The next day Sarah grabbed Ivy as she was running past

her to the kitchen for a mug of water. She had the dreaded scissors in her hand.

"No, ma, not again," Ivy pleaded.

"Get ya arse on that stool and shut ya gob," Sarah ordered. Hair-cutting day was a source of dread to all the kids. Slapping a basin on Ivy's head, she proceeded to cut around it, from the middle of one ear straight round to the middle of the other ear.

Sarah cut all the kids' hair at least once a year, followed by her own, and then Zac. It was the only way to keep the nits down. She then washed their hair in vinegar water.

"It stinks, ma, I smell like fish 'n' chips," Ivy said. Nobody could ever get rid of all the nits, but at least this way you could throw half of them away.

"Go git your sisters," Sarah demanded. Ada and little Sarah suffered the same fate. They both cried. "Shut it. Anybody would think I was killing ya. Now get ya brothers. Go on, hurry up! I aint got all day," she said.

The boys' fate was even worse. They had all the hair cut off, and then Zac shaved their heads. "But Dad, it's so cold me ears might fall off." Herbert whinged. Zac had no sympathy.

"Are you a sissy, boy? Put ya balaclava on, that's what it's for."

A few days later, Zac and Sarah received a summons delivered by the local bobby to appear in the Coalville court. The charge: *Neglecting to send their children to school*. Naming nine-year-old Ivy as the main child of concern.

Mr T G Jesson had been engaged by the court to appear for their defence, who requested the case be adjourned for a fortnight so he could prepare his case.

The request was denied on the grounds that the children needed to return to school, and the case was to be heard a few days later.

Headmaster Henry T Bastard was called to the stand and was asked if he had struck Ivy Parker. To which he informed the court in his large booming voice that he had not laid a finger on the child. Twirling his fingertips around both ends of his stiff moustache. He continued to tell the court that it had been reported to him that a local woman named Bakewell had lost her gold wedding ring. Mrs Bakewell had spoken to one of the schoolteachers, Miss Wright, about this. Later, a daughter of Mrs Bakewell had told him she had passed the ring onto Ivy Parker, who had taken it home.

At this point Mrs Parker stood and said, "Mr Bastard should not have punished Ivy, cause she ain't got the ring ya talkin about."

She was told to sit and be quiet or she would be removed from court.

Ivy Parker was then called to the stand. She said she was eight, nearly nine.

Mr Jesson ask her if she had the ring.

"I never had the ring, cause it had been given to a girl in Thringstone who I don't know," she replied.

She was then asked what happened next.

"Mr Bastard took me out of class and gave me a good hard shaking - hurting my arms and slapping me in the face. He pushed me into a door and all."

According to Ivy. Mr Bastard then told her to go home and not to return again until she brought back the ring.

Mr Rowlett, lawyer for the school, stepped up to ask Ivy a few more questions.

"Ivy, how long do you think Mr Bastard punished you for?"

"Ten minutes," she replied confidently.

"That's a long time, Ivy, how can you be sure?"

"Cos it takes me dad ages in the lavy in the morning. And this was even longer than that."

Fits of laughter were heard from the small crowd, to which the Judge banged on his gavel and called for order.

Sarah Parker was called to the stand, and said her daughter was good and truthful and had attended school regularly.

After deliberation, the bench decided to convict the defendant of failure to send the children to school. And ordered the children return to school the following Monday.

Zac was fined two shillings, and, ten shillings and six pence in costs, which was a heavy fine. Failure to pay within twenty-one days would result in seven days in prison.

It was a few days later when Ivy and Ada returned to school. Mr Bastard eventually admitted thrashing Ivy and apologised to her and Sarah. No more was said on the subject and the ring was never found.

CHAPTER THREE
Trouble and More Court

Over the next couple of years 'The Man Within the Compass' continued as it always had; same crowd, same jokes, same drunks, everyone was happy.

Zac and Sarah managed the pub and punters together. Sarah also tended to the children and the household, as she always had; everything was as normal.

Normal, that was, until the events of Saturday February 14th. The day started the same as any other day. Zac prepared and readied the pub for the evening trade. Sarah organised the children and prepared their tea, which consisted of bread and cheese, and tea, except for little Sarah. She had bread and jam because she didn't like cheese, after which they were all sent off to bed.

Matthew Horne, another regular, secured himself a spot at the bar. He was enjoying the company, and a pint, while keeping a close eye on a small tin box he had placed on the bar.

"Back in a tick, need to piss," Matthew said. "Watch me tin, I won't be long, mines a pint if ya buying." He laughed as he slipped out of the bar. Making his way to the side of the pub. Returning to the bar, Matthew drank his beer, and retrieved his box, opening it to check on its contents. As he looked in, his face reddened slightly, and he called over to

Sarah.

"Which bugger touched me tin box, and helped themselves ta me money?"

"Nobody, Matty. Why, what's up?"

"I had nine shillings in 'ere before I went outside, and now there's only five shilling and nine pence. Who's had me money?"

"Nobody's been near ya box, Matty. Are you sure you had that much in there?"

"Of course I am! Some sod has gone off with me money, and you shoulda kept an eye on it." Matthew's anger was building quickly.

"It was a great deal of money, and now there's only five shillings nine pence left," he repeated.

"I'm sorry Matty, nobody came near ya box and no one's got ya money," Sarah replied, getting annoyed at Matthew's accusations.

"Why did ya bring it in 'ere anyway?"

"It's up to you ta look after it, not me!" she snapped.

"Well, if I can't have all of me money back, I don't want any of it." And with that, Matthew pushed the box towards Sarah at the far end of the bar, and turned towards the door.

As he was leaving Sarah teasingly called after him.

"Well, cheers, Matty, we'll have a great beano with it." A few other regulars had a giggle over this exchange, including Sarah, as she secured Matthew's box from the bar and passed it to Zac. Telling him, "Hold this for Matty, till he calms down and comes back for it." Spinning round to face the whole bar she added, "If, he comes back for it." A few more little giggles and snide remarks were passed around, before the bar returned to the normal Friday activities of drinking, loud conversation and a game of darts.

The next morning Matthew did come back for the money, just as Sarah said he would. She was cleaning the kitchen.

She told him, "Zac has ya money so come back later when Zac was home."

It wasn't just Matthew that came back later that evening, he also brought his wife, Agnes, and his daughter Mary. The hours between the morning, and this evening, had not dampened Matthew's anger on losing his money. He stormed into the bar at around six o'clock with his entourage, and made his way straight to Sarah. Picking up an empty glass, and shaking it towards Sarah, he grimaced.

"Give me back me bleedin money, ya thieving fuckin' bitch." Stunned by his nasty talk Sarah told him to leave.

"I will not stand for that language in 'ere," she bellowed back.

Coming to her father's defence, Mary Horne advanced on Sarah.

"Give me dad back his money, bitch."

Momentarily taken back by Mary's aggressiveness, Sarah took a step backward and repeated, "You all need to leave. NOW! I will not be threatened. I told ya that Zac has your money, and it will be returned to ya."

Mary lunged forward again saying, "If you don't give him back his money now, you will be sorry, ya thieving mongrel."

Taking offense to her accusations and threatening manner, Sarah raised her right hand and struck Mary on her left cheek. There was quite a bit of power in the blow, flinging Mary awkwardly to the floor. She did not move for a few minutes, Sarah, Matthew, and Agnes stood in silence staring down at her, not knowing what to do.

"You've bloody killed her!" exclaimed Agnes bending down to check on her daughter. Just then, Mary opened her eyes, and before she could continue her verbal abuse, Matthew and a couple of the other drinkers lifted her to her feet.

"See I ain't killed her," Sarah said, as she stood herself back up to her full height. "Get her out of 'ere. G'on, you lot, get out of 'ere, and don't come back, ya not welcome 'ere anymore."

With that, Mary stumbled out of the pub with her parents supporting her. Just as Zac was returning and wondering what the hell had gone off here.

Mumblings of, "Police... assault... they will pay..." could be heard as the Hornes made their way out of the pub, and down the road.

"C'mon, Mother, let's get you into the kitchen," Zac said as he tried to bring some normality back to the pub.

"I'm all right," Sarah said as she allowed Zac to lead her into the kitchen.

Sitting her down on a stool Zac smiled and said, "I have a new name for you, Mother. Basher Parker." He said with a smirk. Sarah was not amused.

"Be careful or you will be next."

Still smiling, Zac replied, "You did hit 'er hard, Basher, you could have bloody done 'er in." Sarah looked at Zac and shrugged her shoulders.

"Not my fault she has a face like a smacked arse, and she'll get worse than that if she tries to mess with me again."

"Just be careful now, Mother, she'll probably have the Bobbies round 'ere soon. Best you stop 'ere for a bit and calm down."

"I'll go upstairs and sort out the kids for a bit." Sarah said

Zac turned to go back to the bar. As he made his way out, he called over his shoulder, "I'll go see him tomorrow and give him his box with the money in it."

It didn't take long for the pub to go back to its jolly conversations and friendly banter. Sarah recovered quickly and soon joined in too. Over the next couple of hours, the pub steadily filled with customers, including Danny Price sitting at his regular Friday table, with his scissors and thread. John Robinson, a local labourer made his way into the pub at about seven-thirty p.m. accompanied by his father, William, and brother, Levi.

"Three pints, ta, Sarah," announced William as they made their way to the bar.

"Give us some bread and cheese too," said Levi.

"Bring one for John as well, thanks missus," Levi added, gesturing towards John.

"Right y'are, lads," Sarah replied as she steadied a glass under the beer tap. Sarah placed the three pints on the bar, and then disappeared into the kitchen to organise the two plates of bread and cheese. Dickie Jones, standing next to William joined them into his conversation. "Did you hear 'bout the trouble with Matty Horne and his daughter, Mary?"

"Oh 'aye," replied William. "We did hear summit. Nasty business init?"

"Yeah," Dickie said but bloody good ta watch. "Matty said he lost some money or summit." Dickie held his finger to his lips, signalling to be quiet, as Sarah reappeared from the kitchen with the bread and cheese plates.

"Here ya go, lads." As Sarah turned to make her way back behind the bar, the pub door opened and three young miners made their way inside. "Ay-up, our Joe." Sarah greeted her brother, Joseph Wesley, with a big smile. Turning to his other two friends she said, "Ay-up, Ike. Johnny. What ya 'aving lads?"

"Usual pints, ta sis." Joseph, Isaac Limb and John Parker, Zac's nephew, all worked at the coal mine, clearly evident by the black coal marks on their jackets and hands. Zac made his way back to the bar carrying a couple of empty glasses. He slapped John on the back.

"Ay-up, lad, 'ow ya bin keeping?"

About twenty minutes later, two more local miners entered. Herbert Skellington and James Kearns joining the conversation about Matthew Horne, and the earlier events of the day. "Yeah, news travels fast round 'ere," Herbert joined in.

Police Sergeant Betts came to the pub that night at around eight o'clock. By that time, the pub was full, and the chatter and laugher had fully taken hold. He saw Zac and Sarah, in their element, standing behind the bar laughing, and joking with their customers. He heard small snippets of conversation regarding Matthew and Mary Horne. P.S. Betts contemplated the best way to deal with the issue, having not long since spoken to Mary Horne.

P.S. Betts knew that he would have to approach the subject very soon with Sarah. In a formal capacity.

In the meantime, he was concentrating on what he was there to do, and made his regular surveillance of the pub. Satisfied that all seemed in order, he made his way over to the bar to bid good evening to the landlord and landlady.

"Evening Zac, how be you this evening?"

"Evening, Sarg," replied Zac. "Can I get ya a drink?"

"Just a water ta, Zac. I am here on duty tonight," he replied

"Evening Sarah, I need to have a chat with you, at the station tomorrow morning, officially." A loud chorus of laughter distracted PS Betts, and, as he looked around, he noticed John Robinson slumped near the bar looking like, in his opinion, he'd had sufficient to drink. PS Betts turned back to Zac, taking his glass of water and gestured towards John saying, "Zac, if I were you, I should get rid of him." Zac nodded towards John and told P.S. Betts he'd only had the one pint so far and promised to keep an eye on him. P.S. Betts chatted among some of the other customers, finished his water and left.

A couple of hours later, P.S. Betts returned to the pub accompanied by his partner Police Constable Grewcock. Noticing that John Robinson was still present at the bar, and looking even worse for wear.

P.S. Betts again spoke to Zac. "I'm very surprised to see John still 'ere, seeing as how I already cautioned you when I was 'ere two hours ago."

"He's only had two pints Sergeant, but, as you say I will get him out." Zac turned toward John. "John, lad, I think it's time ta call it a night, you've 'ad your fill." John's father and brother had left about an hour or so earlier, leaving John at the bar with half of his pint left.

Zac made his way to the door in front of John, and held it open for him. John smiled up at Zac, his eyes quite glassy as he stumbled through the door to the street. Losing his balance, John fell down just outside. He picked himself up, took a few more steps and fell again. Witnessing this, P.S. Betts and P.C. Grewcock made their way outside and helped John get up.

"He looks in a bad way, we'll take him home," said P.S.

Betts. "I'm afraid I'll have to report you, Zac, you know the rules," he added, as they both walked past Zac.

Oh great, that's all we need, thought Zac.

One week later, two summons to appear in court were presented to Zac and Sarah. "What's all this?" asked Sarah, as Zac opened the first envelope.

"Looks like I've been summoned," said Zac. Reading further, he explained.

"It's about the night Betts came to the pub and said Johnny was drunk, he said it was my fault for serving him."

"But he wasn't drunk," chimed in Sarah

Reading on, Zac continued. "I'm being charged wi' permitting drunkenness on a licensed premises on February fourteen."

"He only 'ad one pint. Our Joe, Isaac, and James were there, they'll tell 'em!" exclaimed Sarah walking over to stand at the side of Zac, to read over his shoulder. "What's the other one say then?" she asked.

"This one, Mother, is for you, it's for assaulting Mary Horne," Zac said shaking his head. "Better go see Mr Jesson, we will need a solicitor," Zac said, as the events of that night played through his mind.

"God knows what this is all gonna cost" Sarah sighed, close to tears.

A few weeks later, in the middle of March, Zac and Sarah made their way to the local court to face their summons.

John Robinson had also been summoned for being drunk on licenced premises.

Mr George Rowlett prosecuting for the police.

Mr T R Jesson again defended Zac and Sarah. Police

sergeant Betts was called to the stand. Reading from his notes he said, "I entered the Parkers beer house on Loughborough Road around eight p.m. I saw Mr Robinson in the tap room, he had had sufficient to drink, I suggested to the landlord Mr Parker that he should remove him and not serve any more drink to him."

P.S. Betts continued by saying, "Myself and P.C. Grewcock returned to the beer house around ten p.m., and noticed Mr Robinson was still there with a pint glass in his hand, which was half empty." Taking a breath and turning a page of his notes he continued, "Robinson was obviously drunk and could not walk a straight line. I told him to leave and go home, but when he stepped outside, he fell over."

P.S. Betts was excused, and John Robinson was called to the stand.

He said he was not drunk that night, but admitted he had previous convictions for drunkenness.

Sarah told the court she only served Mr Robinson one pint. And all three witnesses Joseph Wesley, brother of Sarah, Isaac Limb, and James Kearns all of Whitwick said Robinson was sober when he left the pub. Another witness, Michael Roach, claimed he saw Mr Robinson leave the beer house, and he walked as straight as a gunshot.

The bench decided that the account from the police sergeant was more likely the truth, especially with Mr Robinson's previous convictions, and that all the witnesses were good friends, or relatives of Mr and Mrs Parker.

Zac was found guilty of allowing drunkenness on his licensed premises, and was fined three pounds three shillings with costs of two pounds six shillings and sixpence, or one month in prison.

John Robinson who was also summoned on a charge of being found drunk on licensed premises, and also found guilty by the bench. John was fined ten shillings with costs of twelve shillings or seven days in prison. Both Zac and John said they would do the prison time. However, the Clerk told Zac that if he chose to go to prison, there would be a distress warrant against his goods. He was then asked again if he wanted to pay the fine or go to prison for thirty days. Zac chose to pay the fine and was given seven days to comply.

As Robinson had no goods that could be seized, he was removed to the cells to commence his seven days in prison.

On the same day, Mr Mathew Horne of Whitwick was summoned for refusing to leave the licenced premises of Zachariah Parker when asked to do so.

Sarah was called to the stand. She said, "Mr Horne asked her to return some money he claimed he lost in the Compass inn the previous evening." She continued, "He threatened me with a glass, and filthy talk. I asked him a few times to leave, but he refused." Sarah was asked what happened next.

"Mr Horne's daughter, Jessie, also demanded the money. When I refused, she scratched my face, I pushed her out of the door. Then Mary and her fourteen-year-old niece started throwing stones at the door."

Miss Horne was then called to the stand. She said, "I called Mrs Parker a thieving bitch, because she wouldn't give back me Dad's money. And Mrs Parker hit me and knocked me out."

At this point, the chairman intimated that the bench had heard sufficient, and the cases against Mr Horne, Sarah Parker, and Mary Horne were dismissed.

Before leaving court, Zac returned Matthew's money box

to his solicitor, as promised, with the five pounds and nine pence inside.

When Zac and Sarah returned home from the court, Sarah put the kettle on stove to boil for tea. Removing her shoes from her aching feet, she said, "We cannot pay your fine, Zac, and the bailiff will be here in seven days with the warrant to take our stuff. I hope he doesn't take my Mam's necklace. It's the only thing I have of hers." Sarah had a sadness in her voice.

As she poured the hot water into the teapot, Zac lowered his voice and said, "Take the necklace to your brother's house till it's all over."

"No! I will not! He'll keep it. He doesn't even know I have it," she replied, hands on hips.

"All right then, hide it in a tin and bury it in the bloody garden." Zac said, his voice starting to raise. "Give it 'ere. I'll do it, you pour the tea." Zac was getting irritated.

"It's not right," she called out as Zac left the room. "Why should we pay because John Robinson gets drunk? He's always bleedin' drunk." Without taking a breath, Sarah continued, "And that copper, Betts, he's just got it in for us."

"Well at least you didn't get a fine, Basher," Zac said slightly sarcastic.

"Zachariah Parker, if you call me that agin, I'll have your guts for garters," Sarah yelled after him as he made his way to the shed in search of a tin box, and a spade.

With all the recent events Zac was seriously thinking of transferring his lease and going back to work in the mine.

"The mine pays regular, and has regular hours, Sarah," Zac reasoned.

"I know but it's not safe. It's only sixteen years ago Whitwick had the collapse, and made a lot of widows."

Zac knew this all too well, he and his Brothers William and Albert, were among the first on scene after the collapse. They were awarded a bravery medal for their efforts. "But the kids are growing now, Ada has finished school, Ivy will finish in December. It will be better all round," he said.

"All right if ya sure, you better go see Mr Jackson at the brewery then." Sarah was sure he was right, besides giving her more time, she wouldn't have to make food for all the customers, and never again have to serve Danny the Taylor. That was a good enough reason on its own

The brewery agreed to Zac giving up his license and on August 14th, 1914, the courts transferred the license to a new landlord and landlady, Albert and Mary Randle. Zac and Sarah moved out the following month.

This was the beginning of a new chapter for the family.

CHAPTER FOUR
Love and War

July 28th, 1914, saw the beginning of four years of sadness, hunger, and broken families. For these were the years of change for Britain.

August of that year also saw the introduction of paper money in Coalville. Consisting of a one-pound note, and a ten-shilling note.

A cause of confusion to many, who were only used to small coins. Sarah was amongst the many who did not like, or want, paper money, not liking change of any kind. It was Zac who said, "This is progress, Mother, you canna stop it."

King George V was seated firmly on the throne. His right-hand man, H. H. Asquith, was Prime Minister until 1916.

However, Britain was no longer the dominant economic power in Europe. Although, it could still boast the largest shipping industry in the world. Coal, iron and light engineering, was now outperformed by Germany.

Young men from all over Britain were volunteering to fight for their country. British newspapers published a very successful campaign, '*Your country needs YOU*', appealing for young men to sign up to fight. Raising a huge volunteer army, which it was hoped would tip the scales in England's favour.

Leicester town hall was a sea of flat caps and straw boaters all vying to add their name to a common cause.

1914 was also the year Zac and Sarah had moved from 'The Man Within the Compass," and settled into a tiny house, still on Loughborough Road, with their five children. It was basic, two bedrooms, a kitchen, and a sitting room.

The sitting room was changed into a bedroom for the three girls. The two boys occupied the smallest room upstairs, and Zac and Sarah the larger room.

The family therefore lived, ate, cooked and washed in the kitchen. Sarah was able to cope with most things life threw at her, while keeping everyone happy at the same time. This was no exception.

Zac had now returned to the mine as a hewer. A particularly back-breaking and dangerous job. He would work six days a week. Entering the mine shaft lift at six a.m. each morning, armed with his pick, and hard helmet with attached lamp.

He held his lunch, usually consisting of bread and cheese, or a homemade cold pie, in a well-worn and dented tin under his arm. For the next eight hours, Zac would be on his back, loosening the coal with his pick, in a shallow tunnel, with only crawl space.

Sarah was now happy that Zac was back in the coal mine, because this was a war-reserved occupation, along with clergymen, farmers, doctors, and iron workers.

Everyone in these occupations were given a certificate, and a badge, stating that they were doing war work, in a reserved occupation, to stem the stigma of cowardice accusations.

She was also pleased beyond words that her sons were not old enough to sign up and go off to war. She could not understand why good men should be fighting, and dying, for someone else's cause. And she was very vocal about this to anyone who would listen.

Their next-door neighbour's sons, Alf, who was just eighteen, and George, twenty-one, had joined the crowd of flat caps, signing up to fight in September 1914.

Sarah comforted Edith, their mother, as the boys turned and waved, before they disappeared from sight. *Why were they smiling?* Sarah thought, *Don't they understand they could be killed?*

A blackout had been ordered in cities, towns and villages across the country. Heavy black curtains, thick cardboard, or black paint had to cover all the windows, and no visible lights were to be left on at night time.

This order included the whole of England. However, the nearby township of Loughborough, consisting of some twenty-five thousand residents, did not initially take the threat seriously, as German bombers had never flown that far inland, so most people in Loughborough had not been concerned.

Including the night of the 31st January, 1916, when at approximately eight p.m. a surprise attack from thirteen enormous Zeppelin airship hovered overhead. The town was entirely unprepared, street lights were blazing, the picture house was lit up to lure cinema goers, and lamps glowed behind curtained windows.

Startled by a succession of loud explosions, the first of which fell in a garden in Orchard Street. Another fell one street away. Luckily missing the gas works.

Moving on, the airships continued dropping bombs on Derbyshire, and Burton-on-Trent. The midlands had been mistaken for the larger town of Liverpool, they were aiming for the docks. Seventy civilians lost their lives that night, countless injured, and many homes destroyed.

After this, no gas streetlights would be lit again until the war was over. And it was against the law to have a light showing in the street, or from a building, at night.

To do so carried heavy fines. Men were employed to walk the streets at night to check for stray lights.

By the end of the War on November 11th, 1918, thousands had been killed on both sides. Zac and Sarah's neighbours had lost both their sons in France the year before the war ended. Edith understandably had been inconsolable, and was rarely seen outside the home, she would speak to no one except the local Vicar, and Sarah. Edith sadly passed away just after the war ended.

By 1921, 'The Man Within the Compass' had a new landlord and Landlady, Mr Seth Wardle, and his wife, Edna.

Seth was a jolly man, with an almost bald head, on top of his chubby round face. His wife often joked that Seth was the only man she knew who parted his hair with a flannel.

Edna was a portly woman, almost as round as she was tall. They had one daughter, Mary, in her late teens. She was a pretty girl, and small in stature unlike her mother.

They had moved to the area to take up the license on the pub, and the locals had taken to the family immediately.

It was on one of those busy nights at 'The Man Within the Compass'.

Sarah, the youngest of Zac and Sarah's girls, named after her mother, was working in the kitchen of the Compass inn. Preparing the food, as her mother had done ten years earlier, when she and Zac had been landlords.

Sarah quite liked working in the pub, and Mrs Wardle was very easy to work for, as long as you worked quickly and quietly. Sarah Parker, was born, and had lived in Whitwick all her life, she had always been sure of herself and what she wanted out of life. She was tall, slim, and had become very confident, a confidence you rarely found in women during the early twenties. She was a pretty woman, with dark wavy hair, a pale complexion, and an infectious laugh.

Sarah had only had a couple of gentleman friends, but no one had really inspired her to want to develop a serious relationship. In fact, none had lasted past a couple of months. The latest of these suitors was Albert. He was four years her senior and worked for his father in the family grocery store. But he was always too busy with paperwork, ordering and serving customers, to actually take some time to court Sarah. Albert's idea of a serious relationship was holding hands in the back room of the grocery store.

He had become increasingly confident that he and Sarah would one day marry. A little too confident for Sarah's liking. *How dare he assume we are anything more than friends,* she had thought.

She often complained about Albert to Mary, Mrs Wardle's daughter, who also worked in the kitchen with Sarah, and sometimes behind the bar.

One night, two strangers entered the pub. One was an older man, and the second, a younger man, who looked around twenty-one years old. Sarah thought they were probably father and son. She could not stop looking at the young man. She peeped through the door cracks, and giggled with Mary.

"If only Albert looked like that." Sarah said, with a faraway look in her eye.

"Come on, girls, git out from under me feet." Mrs Wardle snapped. "Take this steak pie, and bread and cheese out to the two new men in the far corner. And hurry up, girl."

Sarah walked across to where the men were sitting, placed the food down, and looked straight into the eyes of the young stranger.

"Thank you, sir," she said shyly, and felt her face flush with embarrassment.

Walking away, she was sure he was watching her. When she reached the bar, she turned, to see the young stranger was indeed watching her. She flashed a cheeky smile, and found a bounce in her step, as she returned to the kitchen. Sarah was glad that Mrs Wardle hadn't noticed.

"What you smiling about?" Mary asked.

"That new bloke out there, I caught him watching me." Sarah bragged.

"Now girls, leave the customers alone, get on with what ya supposed to be doing." Mrs Wardle said. The next time Sarah had a peep into the bar, she was disappointed to see empty chairs, both men had left.

Sarah's heart sank. She had realised one thing that night. Albert was not the man for her. He had never made her heart race like the young stranger had. She decided that the next time she saw Albert, she would tell him in no uncertain terms that she didn't want to see him again. There was no use prolonging the issue.

All the time she was hoping and praying the young stranger would come back to the pub soon.

She did not have to wait too long, the following week they were back. This time a middle-aged woman accompanied them. Sarah thought it must have been the middle-aged man's wife. Sarah carefully delivered their order to the table, three pints and bread with cheese. This time there was no shyness or embarrassment, Sarah had decided to get the young stranger's attention, she would need to be more mature. Smiling, she placed down the tray, while looking straight at the young man.

"How are ya today?" she asked the young man.

"Busy lass, 'ow bout you?" he replied.

"Well, we should get busy soon," she said, "Better keep going or they will have me guts for garters," she said with a little grin.

Just at that moment, Sarah heard Mary call out, "Can I get a hand 'ere from someone?" Raising her eyes to the sky, Sarah smiled.

"Told you," she said, the stranger smiled back.

"Me name's Isaac by the way."

"Pleased to meet you, Isaac, I'm Sarah, Sally to my friends."

When it came time for them to leave, Sarah was overjoyed to hear Isaac say, "Night, Sally, see you next week."

"Yes, goodnight, Isaac."

Back in the kitchen, Mary was mocking Sally. "Goodnight 'ansome, come back soon 'ansome," she said, laughing.

"Shush," Sally said, as she started wiping the large wooden block in the kitchen. "Get some work done or we'll be 'ere all night."

The next week, Isaac came to the pub alone, Sally was so pleased to see him. This time they talked for quite a while, in between Sally pulling pints for the regulars at the pub, and serving the cheese and bread and steak pies. Before he left for the night, Isaac asked Sally if she would like to go for a walk tomorrow.

"Maybe a picnic?" he suggested.

"Tomorrow good fa me, its Saturday, I only have ta work in the pub in the evening," Sally said.

"I'll pick you up in the morning then. Eleven all right with you?" Isaac asked. "By the way, where do ya live?"

"The grey looking house across the road," Sally replied pointing out of the small window. With that he put on his hat, and was gone.

Isaac Masser Murby was for the most part a very serious man, although he did enjoy a good laugh and good company, his feet were firmly planted on the ground.

Born in the city of Leicester, the nearest city to the little country village of Whitwick, Isaac moved to the village in his mid-teens. He lived with his uncle George and Auntie Eliza, the elderly gentleman and lady who had accompanied him to the pub. He worked on their farm, 'The Hollies', in Swannington. George and Eliza had not been blessed with children but were very close to Isaac.

Isaac was determined to carve out a life for himself, and to one day support a family of his own. He was sure he could do this without too much help from anyone else. Armed with his determination, and his strong sense of right and wrong, a good set of values, and his enormous pride, how could he fail?

Isaac had also decided he liked this little village and knew he would settle nicely here in Whitwick probably for the rest of his life.

Whitwick was a village steeped in history. One of several villages which surround the small town of Coalville. Aptly named because of so many coal mines in the area, which for many years now had been the town's largest industry.

Standing proud in the centre of this town was a newly built magnificent clock tower, complete with a wartime role of honour, containing all the names of the brave men of the area who fell during World War I.

As was the custom in England, there was a public house on almost every corner of the town, and more in the main street leading out of town.

The same was true of Whitwick, in a similar half mile main road, leading away from the village centre, which was called the marketplace, there would be at least four public houses all full of punters in the evenings. At this time there were approximately three and a half thousand residents living in and around the village and thirty-three pubs in total.

Just past the marketplace, was St John the Baptist church, a magnificent stone building, built around 1861, at a total cost of three hundred and eighteen pounds.

Although stone can portray a feeling of coldness, this one seemed strangely warm.

There was small parish cemetery to the right of the church yard, as you entered through the big black iron gates. All parishioners who were of the Church of England faith, were baptised, married, and buried in this church.

Approximately four miles from the marketplace, was Mount St Bernard abbey. A magnificent Roman Catholic, Cistercian Trappist Monastery founded in 1835, one of the first permanent monasteries in England.

The building of the abbey started in 1839, and was consecrated in 1844. Eighty monks and labourers worked for four years, from 1840, to complete the breathtakingly beautiful building of the abbey.

During the build, an excited monk almost broke his vow of silence, as he unearthed a Roman urn containing two thousand Roman coins said to be dated from the third century

AD. A couple of Roman vases, and a spear head was also found next to the urn. All these items found their way to Newark museum.

The monastery was fully maintained by the monks, who were a silent order of self-sufficient vegetarians.

In 1856 a reformatory school for young Catholic delinquents, was founded at Mount Saint Bernard, a total of sixteen hundred and forty boys had been admitted to the school before closing in 1885.

When hard times hit, the monks never turned away anyone regardless of race, colour, or religion and were willing to share what they could. The problem was most of the poor were also religious and would not beg from the church.

It was right next to the monastery that Isaac decided would be a good place for his and Sally's picnic.

At eleven a.m. on the dot Isaac knocked on the back door of Sally's house, she answered, with her coat over her arm, and a basket in her hands.

"What's that ya got?" Isaac inquired.

"Food," Sally said. "We are going for a picnic, aren't we?

"Oh yes, of course we are," Isaac stammered, feeling foolish.

"Bye, Mam," Sally called out, "See you soon."

"Don't be late, 'ome back by teatime!" Her mam called back.

The four-mile walk was slow, and full of conversation. Sally wanted to know everything there was to know about Isaac. She had secretly decided he was the one for her.

She was however a little saddened to hear the reason Isaac moved from the city of Leicester a few years ago was due to a family fallout. She could not imagine falling out with her own family, and actually leaving home because of it. Although sometimes she had threatened it, she never really meant it.

Isaac's family were in the shoe industry, they had a large factory in Leicester, and his father had insisted he learn the trade working his way up the ladder, and maybe one day take over the business with his brother, George. Isaac, on the other hand, had different ideas. He hated the factory, and after a long and nasty feud, he left the family home, which was a modest, detached, brick two-storey house.

His father told Isaac he had washed his hands of him, and never wanted him to return, calling him selfish, and ungrateful. Isaac had no intention of going back.

He told Sarah, "My uncle George has also been an outcast from the family, he took me in, and treated me like a son, I'm very happy there."

Isaac worked hard with George on the farm, he loved it, even in the freezing cold snowy winters.

"Auntie Eliza is a great cook too, she makes her own black pudding, and bread, but her roast beef is the best meal of the week. Every Sunday, right after church," he said, licking his lips.

George had only one fault, and this was a common vice among a lot of men in the towns. George liked a drink, a little too much at times, and pretty regular.

He was not a violent man, drunk or sober, but Eliza was not happy about his drinking. On more than one occasion she had actually hit him with a frying pan or anything she could get her hands on. George rarely even noticed and fell asleep soon after.

It was because of George's drinking, that he and young Isaac ended up in court the following week. George had been summoned for being drunk whilst in charge of a horse and carriage in Ravenstone, and was appearing before The Rev Canon Beaumont.

P.C. Adcock said he saw the defendant with a horse and carriage, his nephew Isaac Murby was with him.

P.C. Adcock continued. "The defendant was leaning with one hand on the splash board of the carriage, while hitting the horse using a cane with the other hand.

"A witness who saw the defendant's condition had told him he was not fit to drive, and suggested he let his nephew drive. To which the defendant had refused."

P.C. Adcock then told the court, "I got onto the carriage and drove the defendant and his nephew home himself. All the way the defendant had to be supported by his nephew because of his condition. When they arrived at the defendant's home he was helped down from the carriage and taken inside."

George was fined five shillings and sixpence, and eleven shillings and sixpence in costs.

This was a lot of money for George to find. The next day Eliza told George that unless he changed his drinking habits, the next time she used the frying pan she would make sure he didn't get up again. Eliza did not speak again to anyone, for almost two weeks. George sold a cow and a horse to a neighbouring farm to pay the fine.

Isaac told Sally about the outcome when he saw her later that week. He was worried she would judge him badly because of George's drinking. He hoped not, because other than that his uncle was a really good and caring man.

To Isaac's surprise Sarah started laughing, she thought it was hilarious.

Isaac and Sally started seeing each other as often as

possible, and their love grew.

He had already decided he wanted to marry Sally but he was very nervous at the thought of going to actually ask her father, Zac.

Sally asked her Mam if Isaac could come for Sunday lunch. Her mother agreed when she saw the pleading in Sally's eyes. She would inform her father they were having a guest for Sunday lunch.

Isaac didn't know it was possible to be so nervous. He was sure he would stutter so much while asking Zac for Sally's hand, that Zac would forbid her to ever see him again.

Sunday lunch was usually meat and potato pie, consisting of mostly potato, covered with a pastry crust, the meat was a lucky dip. Consequently the pie was dry but filling. Today though Sarah had added a few extra pieces of meat in honour of their visitor. Isaac was so nervous, he hardly touched it. Sarah was a little peeved about that.

She asked Sally to help her with the dishes. After giving Isaac a smile and a nod, she slipped into the kitchen. "Does he think I was tryin ta poison im?" Sarah said, hands on hips.

"No ma he was very nervous." Sally was defensive.

"Good, cos I went to a bit of trouble for 'im, glad I didn't kill a chicken now."

Zac offered Isaac a smoke which he gratefully took to calm his nerves.

"Mr Parker," Isaac began, Zac turned to face him. Isaac took a long drag of his cigarette, he started coughing, his face turned bright red, and he wished the ground would open up and swallow him.

Composing himself, he tried again. "Mr Parker," he repeated. Taking a large breath, he blurted out, "Sir, Sally and

I have been seeing each other as you know, for quite a while now." Clearing his throat, he continued. "Mr Parker, I would like your blessing to ask Sally to marry me... Sir."

Zac took a drag of his cigarette, "Mmm you do, do you? Do you love my daughter, Isaac?"

Before he could answer, Zac held up a hand, as if to stop him speaking. Zac continued. "Why would I allow Sally to marry you? What are your prospects young man?" Zac seemed very serious. Throwing question after question.

"Well, sir, I am working as a farm hand at the moment on my uncle's farm, and I love the work, but I am thinking of going down the Whitwick coal mine. There's more money to be made there," Isaac said, very uneasy.

Zac started to laugh, slapping his leg, and rocking backwards. Looking at Isaac's stunned expression he laughed even louder. Sarah and her mother came back into the room, wondering what all the commotion was. "Don't look so worried, lad, of course you have my blessing, she could do a lot worse," Zac said through his laughter.

"Well, Mother" Zac said. "Looks like you may have another wedding to plan."

Isaac turned to Sarah and asked, "Sally will you be my wife? I think I have loved you since the first day I met you."

Sarah smiled as she looked toward her father, who nodded, then turning back she said, "Yes, Ike, yes I will."

Having already married Ada to John Larkin, and Ivy to Cyril Wayte. Zac and Sarah were now preparing to marry off their third daughter.

"Well, Mother, here we go again," Zac said. "The house will seem so empty with just young Zac and Herbert at home."

"Too right, but that means less work for me, and we get a room back," Sarah said with a smile.

CHAPTER FIVE
The First Son

Sally married Isaac Masser Murby, on May 22nd, 1926. Having already decided they wanted a large family was the way to go for them.

Sally was twenty-one years old when she and Isaac exchanged vows.

He no longer worked on the farm with his Uncle George. Having taken a position with the mine, working as coal miner, and doubling as the mine's assistant medical officer.

George and Eliza had taken on a young fourteen-year-old farmhand, straight from school. However, Isaac still made sure he and Sally regularly saw his aunt and uncle.

For the first three months of married life, Sally and Ike had stayed with Zac and Sarah, in the room Sally had once slept in alone, since her sisters had married. During this time Sally became pregnant with their first child.

Ike decided it was time to find a place of their own, and he set about this task with intense enthusiasm.

During August of that same year, Ike succeeded finding a small place they could rent, and begin their life together building a family. The house he found was small but had enough room for both of them and a baby.

Sally came to see the house with excitement, but when she arrived her hand covered her mouth.

"I know this house! Everyone says it's haunted," she said.

Laughing, Ike said, "Don't be silly, Sal, there's no such thing as a haunted house."

She was sure he must be right, but the rumours were convincing.

Anyway, it will be our first home together we must make the most of it, she thought.

'Gunn Hill', as the house was called, looked like a castle, with just one turret, and a flat roof with two tall chimney stacks. Nestled amongst large rocks, looking like it had been carved from them.

The oddly shaped house structure was rather like an upside-down cross. The turret was the centre of the building, with a flat roof. Directly below the flat roof was the one and only bedroom.

Below this was a shared kitchen, eating and living area, which was entered through the front porch. To the left of the kitchen was a small scullery, or wash room, to the right was a tiny parlour, so small you could stand in the middle and almost touch all four walls. Sally now knew were the expression 'can't swing a cat around in here' came from. Outside to the right was a lavatory, and a water pump was near the front of the house.

Sally was not surprised that folk thought it haunted. It was originally built as a gamekeeper's cottage, by a gentleman named Kirby Fenton.

Over the years there had been a few different tenants, Sally and Ike being just the latest.

The house had many legends. One was that a Lord by the name of Giosfrid Aslin had fallen for a young local girl. She did not want to marry the Lord, but her father was so frightened the Lord would take away his livelihood and home, he ordered his daughter be obedient and marry him. She reluctantly did as her father wished. Her life was one of sadness, and heartache. The lord was not kind to his wife, in fact he was cruel, and had also taken to seeing other women.

One day after a particularly hard beating, she ran away, coming upon the Gunn Hill cottage which was devoid of tenants at the time. She stopped and slept there for the night. The next day she was said to have gone down to the nearby pond and jumped in and drowned herself. The legend continued that she liked the solace of Gunn Hill house, and that is why her ghost remains there.

The following week Sally and Ike moved in and settled down to married life together, in their cramped little house, trying to ignore the legends and gossip regarding Gunn hill and the pond.

Over the next seven to eight months, Sally had heard many odd noises, whizzing, creaking and banging. Every time, Ike had to put her mind at ease, saying, "You are listening to the gossips far too much." He suggested she ignore all the talk and get on with life.

One night she woke with a start, hearing a loud, banging noise, and was sure she saw a face at the window. Shaking Ike as hard as she could, she said, "Ike there's someone at the window, get up!" she pleaded. Ike opened his eyes, glanced around the room, and calmly looked at Sally.

"There is no one at the window, Sal, unless they have a bloody ladder. It's just the tree banging on the wall, go back to sleep."

Ike turned over and was asleep before his head hit the pillow. Sally didn't sleep that night, in the morning she checked outside, and the trees around the house.

Ike was right, there was a large tree that was overgrown and touching the bedroom wall. *He must be right, I was being silly*, she thought.

Sally gave birth to their first child, Joyce Sarah, on March 26th, 1927. She was beautiful, and Sally and Ike doted on her. Sally had almost gotten used to the gossip and strange sounds of the house, having rationalised it in her mind, declaring she would have nothing more to do with this nonsense.

Until, one morning, she was washing some of Joyce's baby clothes in the scullery. When a gust of wind whooshed past her, followed by the weight of a hand on her shoulder. Thinking Ike had returned she looked around, but to her amazement there was no one there and the porch door was still closed.

Turning around, her eyes darting to every corner, she began to tremble.

Grabbing Joyce, she fled to her parents' home declaring she would never return.

When Ike arrived to take Sally and Joyce home, she again stated she would not go back to that house. Recounting the events of the day, Ike tried to talk her around, but defeated, he realised this time he would not succeed.

Ike and Sally were not the last tenants to ever live in Gunnhill House. The house deteriorated and eventually collapsed.

A few days later Zac informed Ike and Sally there was a two up, two down house on Loughborough Road for rent. Number 52, just a little way down the road from them.

"It's a row of six terraces," Zac said, "and the end' un just come available, old man Turner, the owner is a friend a mine.

It's yours if ya want it. I think you should take it before some other bugger does," Zac advised.

And take it they did. Moving in wasn't hard as Sally would be happy anywhere other than Gunn Hill. So only thirteen months after moving into Gunn Hill house, the little family was moving out.

"Good riddance to bad rubbish," Sally said when the last box was placed on the horse drawn dray.

She enjoyed setting up their home, hanging a large mirror on the chimney wall and stepped back. *Perfect*, she thought.

The entire building was split into six separate dwellings, each had a front entrance from the main street, and a back entrance. The interior of each of the six dwellings were identical. Six families lived happily alongside each other in this row.

A step up and through the back door, and you were in the kitchen, which was also the dining and daytime living area. Consisting of a sink, an oven, and gas cook top, separated by an open fireplace, a small wooden table, two chairs, and a rocking chair. There was no room for anything more. At the side of this room was a stair case leading up to the two bedrooms. This staircase was hidden by a wooden door.

Underneath the staircase was a tiny pantry which Sally planned to fill with homemade jams, pickles and her famous blackberry vinegar, maybe her mother's potato wine as well.

From here, there was another step up into the best room, a bigger room by maybe three feet, but still very small. Both rooms had a mirror hanging on the wall over open fire places, which would be burning winter and summer alike. This was the only way there would be hot water, and warmth.

Coming in from the front entrance, led straight into the

best room while the back entrance led directly into the kitchen. Just outside the back door was a coal shed, more of a lean to, but served the purpose of storing and keeping the coal and wood dry.

Upstairs were two bedrooms identical in size and shape to the two rooms below them. The smaller bedroom above the kitchen had a cot for Joyce and a small wooden wardrobe. The larger bedroom above the best room had a double bed, and a larger wooden wardrobe.

The garden to all six dwellings stretched the width of the building, and approximately three hundred feet in length. This was split equally between the six families, and was called an allotment. The tenants could grow whatever they wanted on their allotment.

At the opposite end of the building from Sally and Ike's house, there was an entry leading from front of the terraces to the back entrances of all the dwellings, rather like a train tunnel. The toilet however was also at this opposite end of the building, just past the tunnel. Sally and Ike had to walk the full length of the building to use the toilet, in all weathers. There were only two toilets, one toilet for three households. So you could run down there in the rain or snow, and, if it was occupied, there was no shelter. Either you would get absolutely soaking wet while waiting, or you ran back and try again later, if you could hold on that long.

Sally however had placed a guzunder pot under the bed for when taken short during the night. She was not walking down there in the dark, with just a candle for light.

September 4th, 1928, in the early hours of the morning. New life was about to start, a second child for Ike and Sally. Born in the same idyllic little village in the heart of England that Sarah had been born, twenty-three years earlier. And Joyce just a year ago.

"Ike wake up, its time," Sally was pulling, and slapping Isaac's arm. "Ike wake up," she said again.

"Ruddy hell, woman. What is it? What's up Sally?"

"It's time Ike, the baby is coming."

Sally knew the signs, just as she had known she was pregnant nine months earlier, before the doctor confirmed her condition. After all, sixteen months ago Sally had given Ike a beautiful daughter, after an easy pregnancy and a relatively easy birth.

"Are you all right, me duck?" Ike asked Sally, dragging his pants from the nail they were hanging on, in the middle of the bedroom door. He pulled them on, flicking his braces over his shoulders.

"Shall I go fetch Mrs Bridges?" Ike asked.

"Yes, I think you should." Sally said as another pain came.

"Will you be all right?"

"Yes," Sally said." I'll be right, just go I'm fine." And she was. Sally wasn't easily scared, if you don't count Gunn Hill House. She was quite confident she would be fine. The pains were about ten minutes apart, so she knew she had plenty of time.

Sally thoughts drifted wondering if she would have a boy this time. Something she had pondered quite a few times over the last nine months. Most of all hoping it would be healthy no matter what it was.

"Please God, let it be healthy," she said aloud, knowing Ike would love a son, but another daughter wouldn't be bad either. *Wouldn't it be nice if you could find out the sex of your child before it's born? Then you could have everything ready that would be really nice.* Her thoughts trailed as another wave of pain jolted her back to reality. The pains were getting closer together.

"Come on Ike, hurry," Sally said to herself.

With the next surge of pain, Sally felt her waters break. Now she knew it was getting very close. Ike burst into the room, with Mrs Bridges in tow, and out of breath.

"Aye-up, Mrs Murby," she said panting and gasping for air, "You know just when t' go into labour don't ya? Third time this week I've been called from me bed. Well now, no time for niceties, let's get down to it. 'Ow far apart are your pains?" Mrs Bridges inquired.

"Only a minute or two," Sally blurted out, as another pain took hold.

"Waters broken, I see." Mrs Bridges stated

"Yes, just a few minutes ago."

Still as bossy as ever, she never seems to stop for breath, always been a bossy woman, do this, do that, I wish I could manage without her, Sally thought.

Mrs Bridges was around fifty-five years old, but no one knew her age for sure. She had salt and pepper hair, more salt these days, a double chin, with spiky hairs, which wobbled when she moved her head, and round rim glasses perched on the end of her long, fat nose, adorned her stern and serious face,

It was almost like she had never smiled in her life. Maybe she had never had any good reason to smile. Although, you would think helping to bring new life into the world would be reason enough.

Mrs Bridges was quoted once as saying, "It's quite depressing to think all these beautiful babies, will just have to make do in life with what they can git."

She was always full of advice for everyone. And whether you wanted it or not, you got it. Including advice on how to bring up children. And how folks should try to avoid having large families that are always hard to feed, and clothe.

"Mr Murby, don't just stand about, I will need hot water, and clean towels right away." Mrs Bridges barked, clapping her hands together.

Mrs Bridges didn't have any children of her own, in fact she was never married. Everyone called her Mrs Bridges to be respectful and polite. Her first name was Elsie, but no one ever used it.

Ike brought up the hot water, and a couple of clean towels. After checking Sally was all right, he left the room as quickly as possible. He checked on Joyce who was sleeping soundly in her cot, then headed straight down the stairs to the back door. After pacing up and down, which seemed the customary thing for a father-to-be, he sat down on the cold stone step that Sally scrubbed clean almost every day and lit a cigarette.

He felt like he had been sitting there for an eternity, his bottom was certainly cold and numb, when he heard the squeal of a new life; a new life he was now responsible for. He wondered if this one was a boy, or another girl. Remembering hearing the lads at work one day saying, "It takes a man to produce a girl. It's a well-known fact," they said. "Men determine the sex of a child, and strong men have more girls." Well, he thought, another girl wouldn't be too bad really.

"MR MURBY!" yelled Mrs Bridges.

God! he thought she sounded like an old fisher woman, *No wonder she never found anyone willing to marry her.*

"MR MURBY! Where are you? Come and see your new

son."

"A son!" he said as he ran up the stairs two and three at a time. Peering in through the door, he saw Sally lying comfortably in bed, holding their new son. His heart was fit to burst.

"What a lucky man I am," he said.

He had never seen Sally look so beautiful. Moving to her side, he sat on the chair next to the bed.

"'Ere Ike, hold your son." Sally said, passing the baby over.

Looking down at the tiny face Ike said, "He's perfect. Sally. We have to give him a name. What do you think?"

Sally thought for a while, then said, "I think Desmond Isaac might be nice."

"Yes, I like Desmond," Ike said, but he preferred it the other way around.

"But I prefer Isaac Desmond." Just a mere formality, he thought.

"No!" Sally said. "Desmond first is far better, with his dad's name in the middle." And with that the discussion was over.

Just in time to save a disagreement, they heard a child cry. Looking over at Desmond, to see he was sound asleep, they realised it must be Joyce. In their excitement they had forgotten all about her. And she had slept through the whole thing. "We should introduce her to her new brother." Sally said. Ike went into her bedroom and found her, arms outstretched.

"Aye-up there," he said. "Come and see what we have for ya."

Returning to Sally and Desmond, he leaned over to show

Joyce her little brother. She wasn't interested, she just cried, and wanted her Mam.

"All too much for you." Sally said, giving Joyce a cuddle and before long she and Sally were both fast asleep.

"Well," said Ike, "I think I might put the kettle on. What about you Mrs Bridges, would you like a cup a tea?"

"That's sounds very nice thank you Mr Murby." Mrs Bridges said. "But make sure the kettle boils properly, canna have a good cuppa if the water ain't boiling."

"Yes," Ike said, his voice trailing, as he walked down the stairs.

The next day Ike went to town to register the birth of his first son. First son because both he and Sally wanted a large family, so Ike was sure Desmond would not be his last son.

Once inside the registrar's office he started to fill out the forms. Father's name, mother's name, maiden name, sex of child. Then he came to the child's name. He stopped. Looking around the room rather like a cheeky little boy. He said aloud, "Child's name…" and very quickly wrote 'Isaac Desmond'. The birth was recorded, and certificate issued. "Oh well, it's too late now," he whispered to himself. He knew he would still be called Desmond, but he would know his first name was really Isaac.

Besides, no one ever looks at birth certificates anyway, he reasoned, *as long as you have one that's all that counts.*

Over the next ten years, Ike and Sally welcomed four more children, all boys. So Ike had been right, he knew there would be more sons.

April 1932 saw the arrival of Herbert George, June 1934 came Norrice. Two years later in 1936 Derek Brian was born, followed in 1938 by Ike and Sally's last child, Norman

Michael.

So with a daughter and five sons, the family was now complete. And Mrs Bridges, who delivered them all, was able to retire in the knowledge that her services were no longer required in the Murby house.

Ike prayed all six of their children would grow up in the knowledge that their parents loved them all equally. And if nothing else in this world, he hoped they would always be able to depend on each other.

CHAPTER SIX
Teenage Boys

The family may not have had too much in the way of wealth, very few had more than they needed, and some not even that.

But the six Murby children were brought up to be well mannered, to do as they were told, and to always watch out for each other.

Ike had been a member of the St John's Ambulance brigade for a few years, joining as a young man. He had worked his way through to the senior level, and became Superintendent of the Coalville division, on Forrest Road. Using this knowledge, he was promoted to chief medical officer at the mine.

Friends and neighbours would always knock on his front door with headaches, cuts, bruises and sometimes worse. It was quicker and easier to come to Ike than to go to the doctor, and Ike bandaged and cleaned their wounds perfectly.

In return they gave him eggs, homegrown cabbages, runner beans and apples as a thank you, all of which were very welcome, because rationing had hit the people of England hard.

Sally however, had her own cures for certain things. Blue bag she used for bee stings, even though its proper use was for keeping white linen white in the wash, Olive oil she used slightly warmed, for ear ache. Butter for burns, and she would rub dock leaves on blisters from stinging nettles. Her homemade blackberry vinegar was a winner for sore throats, it tasted horrid but seemed to work like a charm.

Rationing was in place in Britain as a means of ensuring the fair distribution of food and commodities when they were scarce. It began after the start of WWII with petrol, and later included other goods such as butter, sugar and bacon. Ration books were given to everyone, who then registered with local shops of their choice. Sally and Ike were registered with their local butcher, baker and greengrocer, they had been given ration books and coupons for food for the family. Each person's weekly allowance was, one egg, two ounces of butter, two ounces of tea, one ounce of cheese, eight ounces of sugar, four rashers of bacon, and four ounces of margarine.

She would give some of their bacon rations to other families in the row with children when she could, because the family was lucky to have pigs and hens. She was very grateful Ike was vigilant with breeding the animals, thankful for his green thumbs, and the vegetables he grew in his allotment.

Ration points that were unused and saved, could later be redeemed to purchase non-rationed goods like cereal, tinned food, biscuits, dried fruit which although not rationed, were expensive.

It was a rarity for the children to have sweets, Sally kept this as a special treat for birthdays and Christmas.

When the runner beans were in season, Sally would salt them in large jars, to store for winter. Her favourite vegetables were brussel sprouts, known as knobs grown in winter, which were only good after they had a frost on them. She would snap a stick off and there would be up to twenty large knobs on each stick.

Ike's friend, Albert, suggested they join the Whitwick colliery home guard. They could work together, doing their bit for the war effort. Both were reserved occupation working at the mines during the day, coal was still a much needed commodity. But, protecting the streets, and ensuring blackout was observed by everyone to avoid being seen, and possibly bombed by Hitler's planes, was important too. And so Ike and Albert became the newest members of the home guard.

Leaflets had been delivered, and posters had been nailed to trees, fences, schools, and churches. Informing everyone including the children, of the precautions and procedures for schools during an air raid:

Firstly, your gas mask must be with you at all times. Never leave home, or school, without it. If you are on your way to school and the siren sounds, run to the nearest sand-bag shelter, or police box. Failing this, the nearest house.

All schools have been provided with adequate specially constructed air raid shelters. When an air raid siren sounds, the children must immediately be taken to the shelter. Parents are requested not to try to collect their children from the school during a raid.

One by one the men in the area seemed to be going off to war either by volunteering, or the dreaded conscription.

Far too many of these brave men would not be coming home.

Every woman dreaded the sight of the telegram boy on his bicycle.

And although they all rallied around a grieving family,

they were happier to see him cycle past their homes.

All of the Murby children attended school until the age of fifteen, except Joyce. She was the only one to finish school at fourteen, before the leaving age was amended to fifteen. Her schooling ended in 1941, two years after the start of WWII. She helped her Mam with the housework, and her younger siblings.

By the end of 1943 Desmond was ready to leave school and enter the adult world of working for a living. He was a very bright lad. His teachers had spoken to Ike on more than one occasion, saying he should be allowed a higher education. Desmond was interested in weights and measures. The units and standards for expressing the amount quantities, such as length, capacity, or weight; the science of measurement.

The training however was very expensive, and Ike agonised over this for a couple of weeks. One of Desmond's teachers Miss West came to the house to talk to Sally and Ike on this very subject. She had a soft spot for Desmond and thought he had the potential to excel in weights and measures, and informed them that Desmond had already been offered a place and training in this field.

Ike and Sally could not afford to send Desmond for this training because, as was explained to Desmond, "You have four more brothers growing up, and I cannot do this for you, son, if I cannot do it for the rest." Desmond was disappointed but understood and accepted what his father had said. So after leaving school he headed to the coal mine with his father.

Ike was the mine's Medical Officer (MO) and Desmond became his assistant, having passed all his first aid and home nursing exams.

Desmond had followed his father and become a member

of the St John's ambulance, he often practiced on his mother, especially when he had an upcoming exam, he would wrap her in bandages, and reduce his siblings to fits of laughter.

He was placed in the senior division with Ike. Both men enjoyed the brigade, and marching through the streets, behind the Salvation Army band at Christmas, Easter and Armistice Day, ending at the church for special services. Desmond knew all the hymns by heart, and Ike could hear him singing above everyone else.

He loved the time he spent with his father, it was his personal time, time he did not have to share with the others. Both men would remain in the brigade for many, many years.

1944 came and went very quickly, Ike now had four pigs and eight piglets on his allotment. Breeding them was a lot of work. The neighbours helped with food by saving all the potato peeling. Any peelings and scraps fattened them up.

Three or four times a year Tom Broadhurst, the butcher, came to kill and prepare the meat. After which a side of bacon was hung in the kitchen. The boys would slice a piece off and throw it into the pan.

As well as the pigs, Ike bred chickens, having around twelve to twenty at any one time. They were bantam chickens, a miniature version of regular chickens. Sometimes he sold a few for extra cash, especially when he was getting a few too many to handle.

When a special occasion loomed, the boys would gather outside the back door, around a large round tin bath, to pluck and gut the chickens, tearing out the feathers by the handful, and tossing them into the tin bath. Gutting was a job done a little slower, the boys had been taught how to do this expertly.

If the liver had a funny green looking sac attached, it was

the gallbladder. This would need to be removed without rupturing it, and discarded quickly, as it was filled with bile and if it burst, it would give the meat a bitter taste.

Ike was always careful to ensure the live chickens were safely locked in their coop at night, in case the foxes came calling again, as they had once before.

Ike also loved canaries and bred them too. He had built two sheds to hold his precious canaries. Each shed had approximately eighteen to twenty cages in rows above each other, and a bird, sometimes two, in each cage. Ike loved them, and tended to them twice a day, morning and night. He would hard boil eggs, and mix them with chickweed, a small green leafy plant, every morning and seeds at night.

Sally always said those birds were treated better than she was, but Ike knew she didn't mean it.

Sometimes when he could, he would take the birds to shows, or a fellow canary lover would take them for him. His birds won many ribbons, those days were especially pride filled days. One day, one of his canaries won the best in a show and was named the champion, at the biggest show in Britain. Ike was asked to represent England in the next show in Scotland, but he declined, because it was too far to travel, and he could not afford the time, the train fare or the entry fees. And anyway, he knew his birds were all champions.

Sally worried sometimes Ike was spreading himself far too thin.

To help out, the boys had decided they would be the self-appointed designated hunters. Their job was to bring home food for the table. Setting traps in the fields at night, they would return early the next morning to see what they had caught.

Desmond, Norrice and Herbert also hunted with ferrets, and a grey mongrel called Toby. Desmond put the ferrets inside his shirt, which was tucked into his trousers. The ferrets ran around his middle freely.

Finding a rabbit hole, a ferret was dropped into the hole to chase the rabbit out. The boys would be waiting at the other end, with a sack to catch the rabbit. Then Desmond caught his ferret and put it back into his shirt.

Sometimes they would take the family shotgun and shoot a couple of pigeons. One of Desmond's favourite dinners was pigeon pie, and Sally was expert at cooking it with spuds and gravy. Sally was expert at cooking anything.

"'Ere ya go, Ma. Summut for the pot tomorrow," they would say very proud of their contributions.

One day, Norrice and young Norman had gone out hunting, Norrice thought he would teach his young brother the ropes. "Come on, our kid, hurry up." Norrice called out, Norman ran to catch up, carrying the sack for their spoils.

A loud and violent storm the previous night had left everywhere saturated. After trudging through wet grass and mud, for what seemed like forever, the rain started again. The two lads decided it was too hard in the miserable and wet weather, and abandoned the hunt. Not wanting to return empty handed they hatched a plan.

Zac, the boy's grandfather, often called in to visit the family, but today he brought with him his friend of many years, Edwin the local bobby, for a cup of tea, and to get out of the rain.

Norrice and Norman returned drenched to the bone, and threw the sack onto the table, "For the pot, Ma," Norrice said, looking around quite proud. Then he noticed the bobby and his grandfather. Gulping, he tried to stop his Mam from opening the sack, but, too late she tipped the sack, and out came two black and white fluffy rabbits.

"They are the best-looking WILD rabbits I have ever seen, Ike," said the bobby.

Zac agreed, and both men burst into fits of laughter.

When Zac and Edwin had left, Ike pulled on his work boots. The lads knew what was coming. Ike hated stealing of any kind, and he kicked both lads' bums all the way to the bottom of the allotment leaving them out in the pouring rain to think about what they had done.

Tuesday morning, Sally sighed. Wash day, she hated wash day. The heavy lifting, and keeping the fire going too, was no mean feat. Sally and two of her neighbours Mrs Benson and Mrs Campbell, shared the washhouse. And the same three families also shared one toilet as well.

Sally put on her full-length wrap-around apron, as she did every morning.

She called out to Joyce to shake a leg and stop wasting time. It was their turn for the washhouse today, so she knew she could not put it off until tomorrow. Rain, hail or snow, if it was your turn, you had to take it, or miss out.

The washhouse was a smallish square room, which consisted of two concrete troughs for hand washing and rinsing. Sally would wash her and Joyce's bloomers, and Ike and the boy's shirt collars by hand every week, then starch the collars before drying, giving a nice stiff collar. Desmond always complained that they were so stiff it hurt his neck.

There was also a large cast iron copper with a metal lid, and a metal area underneath the copper, where the log fire would blaze and boil the water.

It would take twelve to fourteen full buckets of water from the water pump, which Joyce now collected these days, to fill the copper to the desired depth. Then Sally would light the fire, wait twenty minutes for the water to boil.

Then, using her copper stick she loaded the sheets, and any whites, adding the blue bag for whiter whites.

While they were boiling, she used her plunger pushing it up and down on the sheets. This was particularly hard as the copper was quite large so to do this, Sally would need to stand on a large stool so she could see inside and get the height to give the washing a good plunge. Sometimes she burnt herself on the boiling water.

Using her copper stick, she then lifted the sheets straight across into the rinsing trough, where Joyce would then put them through a hand rolled mangle and then out to peg onto the wash line.

Next was towels and colours, same routine and more wood on the fire. The last to be washed was Ike and the boys' work clothes, and anything worn when hunting and gardening. By this stage the water was a filthy dark brown colour and nothing else could be put in there so Joyce would use the bucket to empty the copper tipping all the water down the sink.

The washing would dry quickly if it was a windy day, if not, it was clothes horses round the fireplaces in both rooms. December and January were the worst, Joyce hated getting in the washing when it had frozen into stiff boards. The sheets and towels would crack when trying to fold them to carry into the house and bend them over the clothes horse.

When the washhouse was cleaned ready for the next person, it was time to start dinner. Then to iron the now washed clothes and sheets.

Both Sally and Joyce were always glad of their beds on wash day. Joyce often sang the children's wash day song if it was a particularly wet day:

Rain, rain, go away,
Come again another day.

For Joyce, the wash day rain did go away, she was to start work at Tomlins shoe factory in Shepshed. She was very happy to be going out to earn a living like the men, and some of her friends.

The day after wash day was shopping day. Sally and Joyce needed to get milk, flour, Ike's tobacco, and a few other essentials, and drop off six dozen of the bantam's best eggs, which the shop keeper sold for Sally, to his customers.

"I wish we didn't have to walk all the way home with these heavy bags," Joyce complained.

"Shanks's Pony is good enough for me, so it's good enough for you, God gave ya legs to use, now get a move on," Sally said.

When they returned home, the kitchen was a mess, black soot everywhere.

"What on earth!" Sally stopped, realising what the problem was.

"Get water on the stove to boil, and pass the broom Joyce, the chimney soot has fallen," Sally said with a sigh.

"I told ya Dad it needed sweeping, before it caught on fire, like Mrs Rosen down the road, that was a big un ten-foot flames coming out the chimney pot. Now look at this mess."

She was not happy. The woman spent two hours scrubbing and sweeping and scrubbing some more. That night's supper would be bread and dripping, and a bit of cheese, and if anyone dared to complain, Sally was ready. When Ike and the boys saw Sally's facial expression, no one dared to complain. And they all ate their small meal like it was a banquet fit for a king.

CHAPTER SEVEN
Life and Death

Mr Jones, the chimney sweep, arrived on Saturday morning, laden with all his brushes and extendable sticks.

"Mornin' misses," he said to Sally.

"Aye up, Mr Jones."

"Shall I start in the kitchen, or the best room?" he asked.

"The kitchen, thank you, I need to cook later," Sally retreated upstairs to make the beds.

Putting a large cloth over the fireplace in the kitchen to cover the entire fire space, the mantel, and a good portion of the floor. He proceeded to push his large, stiff, round brush up the chimney. Attaching another stick by screwing it to the previous one, he pushed it up even higher. He did this maybe four or five times, until the brush came out the top of the chimney pot on the roof.

Looking at young Norman, who was fascinated by the process, he said, "D'hear lad, trot outside and tell me if you can see me brush on the roof." Norman ran outside and was amazed he could see the brush waving about above the chimney pot.

Running back inside he yelled, "Yes, mister, I saw it!"

"Good," said Mr Jones, "I'll pull the little blighters back down then."

When he removed the cloth, the hearth was full of soot,

which he proceeded to clean up and tip into his bucket. "Now then lad, I better do the other chimney in the best room, you can help again by telling me when it pops out the pot on the roof." Norman was only too happy to oblige. He went outside and waited and waited until the brush again popped out the chimney pot.

When all was done, Mr Jones said to Sally, "You were lucky. If you left it any longer misses, you'd 'ave had a chimney fire." Sally knew he was right and took a half-crown from her purse to pay him. Then Mr Jones tied all his sticks and brushes to his bicycle and went on his merry way, whistling a merry tune.

A short time later Desmond was brought home by his buddies, Malcolm and Peter, "Misses, where's Mr Murby? Desmond's bin bitten by that bleedin ferret," Peter said.

"Watch ya language, me lad, unless you like the taste of soap," Sally replied. "Ike is down the allotment, Peter go get him," she continued.

Getting some water, she told Desmond to take off his shirt, and proceeded to clean the bite, while Desmond squirmed in his seat.

"Let's 'ave a look, lad," Ike said as he walked through the back door. "A bit of disinfectant and a plaster is all you need."

"But it really hurts," Desmond insisted.

"You should be more careful, you'll have worse than this afore ya die, lad," Ike said unsympathetically. "Now put ya shirt on and go feed the chickens, like you were supposed to this morning."

Ike was serious and Desmond knew it. "Okay, Dad," Desmond said obediently.

Joyce had slept in the corner of her parent's room since

the boys had taken over the small bedroom, which was overflowing, with five boisterous boys.

She was no longer happy sharing with her parents, and often wondered why they couldn't get a larger house, or at least let her sleep in the best room behind the kitchen. However, Sally had said that it was not possible to move, and none of her business.

"You can't always have what you want, or I would be swanning around the palace," Sally said.

But to appease the situation a little, Sally put up a large curtain in the bedroom, splitting the room in two so Joyce could have more privacy. It was not ideal as far as Joyce was concerned but it would have to do for now, and Joyce knew it wasn't worth fussing any further.

Very early one morning, around four a.m., Ike and Sally were jolted awake by the boys arguing with each other again.

"Shift over, Herbert!" someone shouted.

"I did!" came a reply.

"Stop kicking me, or you'll be sorry!" Desmond said.

"Just try it, go on I dare you," Norris taunted. Norman was crying because he claimed someone kicked him in the stomach.

Hearing Desmond march downstairs to sleep on the couch in the best room, Ike had heard all he cared to.

"ENOUGH!" Ike yelled, "Or I will bang all your bloody heads together and Norman stop that crying, or you will git summut to cry for!" Ike was getting angry because he had to get up soon to feed the animals. "Now go back to sleep. I don't want to hear another peep!" Ike threatened.

When Ike came home from work that night, Sally suggested they buy a second-hand single bed and add it at the boy's room.

"It will fit nicely, and then Derek and Norman can top and tail, the other three will have more room in the double bed. What do you think?" Sally was looking at Ike for approval, she knew he would agree, he always did.

Ike wasn't silly, he knew Sally made most decisions around the house. So a few days later a single bed arrived and the boys were happy and promised no more arguments. "There better not be or I'll take it away again," Ike warned.

It was a cold wet day, one of many lately. Sally was on her way up the road to visit her parents as she did couple of times a week.

"Ay-up, Sally, glad you are here today," Zac said. "Your Ma isn't well at all, she has been in bed a couple days now. See if you can cheer her up," Zac said concerned.

Sally entered her parent's room and asked her mother how she was feeling. Sarah looked pale and completely worn out. "Have you eaten anything, Ma?" Sally asked.

"Not hungry," was all Sarah could reply.

Sally patted her mother on the hand and told her she would return in a few minutes.

"Why didn't you tell me sooner, Dad?" Sally scolded Zac.

"She wouldn't let me because you have enough to do," Zac said.

"Dad, I can send one of me boys to ask the doctor to call in today?" Sally was worried. She had heard of people becoming sick lately, and quickly going downhill, with no return to good health.

Sally warmed some soup, and made a cuppa, trying to help Sarah to eat something, but Sarah only managed three spoonfuls of soup, and none of the tea.

Herbert came to the house telling his mother that the doctor was on his way.

Doctor Stevenson arrived about ten minutes after Herbert, and was shown to the bedroom where Sally sat with her mother. Doctor Stevenson examined Sarah, using the usual none committal tones doctors seem to practice. Finally he spoke. "We will need to get Mrs Parker to the hospital, so we can do more tests. I will however tell you, I am very concerned for your mother's health at the moment."

Sally started to move Sarah so they could put on her coat and slippers. But Sarah gave out a loud cry and flopped into Sally's arms.

"Doctor, Doctor help me," Sally called out, just catching the Doctor as he was leaving the room.

Rushing back into the room with Zac close on his heels, he lay Sarah back down and put his stethoscope in his ears listened to Sarah's heart.

After a few anxious moments. Doctor Stevenson stopped and looked at Zac.

"I am so sorry, Mr Parker, but your wife has passed away, I think Mrs Parker has suffered a heart attack. My sincere sympathies, sir."

Doctor Stevenson continued, "I will see the undertaker is informed. Is there anything I can do for either of you before I leave?"

"No, thank you Doctor, we will be fine." Zac saw the Doctor out the door, and turned, to find Sally standing behind him. Zac put his arms around Sally.

Hugging each other they cried a bucket full of tears. Sally told Herbert to go tell Norrice to fetch his aunt Ivy, and his aunt Ada. And tell Desmond to get his uncle Zac and his uncle

Herbert.

The undertaker came and gently placed Sarah in the hearse, Sally and her sisters cleaned the house and changed the bedsheets. While Sally's brothers took care of Zac. Each one tried to be brave, in the light of the distressing, and sudden death of their mother.

Ada insisted Zac should stay with her and her husband John, until after the funeral, and all agreed that was best. Sally was in a daze when she told Ike what had happened. She broke down again, saying, "I thought Ma would live forever, it's not her time yet!" Ike supported Sally through the worst, and through the funeral.

Zac, Ada, Ivy, Sally, Zac Jr. and Herbert were the first to arrive at the church, followed by all Sarah's grandchildren, other relatives and friends.

It wasn't a lengthy service, the vicar was kind in his address, and spoke about Sarah as if he knew her well. Zac Jr. spoke on behalf of the family.

"Our mother was a hard working woman, who never ask for anything that did not benefit her family. We love her, and will miss her for the rest of our lives. We thank her for making us strong, independent people. And promise her we will always be there for our father." Wiping a tear, Zac Jr. then placed a pink carnation on Sarah's coffin. His siblings did the same, followed by the grandchildren.

Sarah was taken to the local cemetery and buried with just family in attendance. There were enough tears shed to fill a well. The loss of Sarah would be felt for a very long time.

Life slowly moved on, and Zac moved into a two roomed dwelling a few doors down from Sally and Ike. This made Sally happy that she could keep a closer eye on her father, and his health. Every day she included Zac in the meals she cooked, and would walk to his home each day to deliver the food.

Zac had no interest in going anywhere other than his piece of garden. Ike had given him a few bantams to keep him interested in something, and Zac liked to collect the eggs. Apart from this, all Zac would do was read, that was now his life.

"Morning, misses," came a familiar voice through the kitchen window. "Where do you want it then?"

Sally looked up from the table where she had been drinking her cup of camp coffee.

"Oh, morning, Cyril, in the shed will be fine thanks, fancy a coffee?" Sally asked.

"Ah that's the best idea I've heard today, Let me get the other three bags of coal then I'll be with ya," he replied, tipping the contents of the coal bag expertly over his shoulder into the coal shed. Coal was the main source of fuel for households and industry. Because Ike was employed by the coal board, he received a heavy discount on his coal.

Cyril wiped his boots at the door. Sally put some newspaper on the chair, so he could sit down, without dropping coal dust that Sally would have to clean up later. Picking up his cup of coffee he wrapped his heavily coal stained hands around it, as if to warm himself. "Ah, that's grand, misses, hits the spot," Cyril said.

"You're welcome. Got many more deliveries today?"

"Half dozen is all, then load up for morning." Cyril seemed tired, the life of a coal delivery man was a back-breaking job. Not only did Cyril have to deliver four large bags to each house on his list, but on his return to the coal yard he had to re-fill all the large empty bags, and load the truck ready for the next day's deliveries.

He finished his coffee and stood up, tipping his hat, he thanked Sally and left, Sally heard him singing, "*I'm looking over a four leaf clover, that I overlooked before,*" all the way to the entry tunnel.

Sunday was called the day of rest, Sally always said there's no rest for the wicked. Sunday came around very quickly, too quickly, Sally thought, but there was still work to be done She knew that after church everyone needed something to do, so as not to get under her feet.

Ike was putting his boots on, He was going down the bottom of the allotment to see to the animals, he was complaining about what a long way it was to the bottom of the allotment, when you have to carry everything, backwards and forwards. He was taking Derek and Norman with him today. They could carry the pig feed and do some digging and planting. Sally sent Herbert down to her father's house, to help his grandad tend his small garden and feed the chickens. Joyce would help Sally cook and clean. Desmond and Norrice had gone out straight after church, hunting rabbits with three sacks this time. They must have been feeling optimistic.

The boys thought it would be good to walk further afield, they thought they might get some blackberries as well, knowing their Ma would be pleased, and could make a lovely pie for pudding.

Norrice threw a stick and Toby as usual retrieved it, "That dog's bloody mad, Desmond, just like his owner," Norrice said, just as a wet cow pat flew past his head.

The hunt was a good one, two wild hare, three pigeons and blackberries. "We got a bloody ton of berries today, our kid," Desmond said.

"Sure did, but Ma will make that horrible blackberry vinegar, I bet ya," Norrice said.

Laughing, Desmond agreed, reminding Norrice, "It's bloody good for ya throat."

On the long walk home, the boys notice a building site. A new row of houses similar to the one they lived in, was being built. Being Sunday, no one was around, so the boys went in for a closer look.

Stacks of bricks were piled about three feet high, there were tons of sand, and two wheelbarrows. The wheelbarrows were well used and a bit on the rusty side, dried concrete lining the inside. Desmond raised his eyebrows at Norrice and Norrice nodded. Each knew what the other was thinking. Quickly getting to work, they loaded bricks into the wheelbarrow threw the three sacks on top, and took turns wheeling all their spoils home. "Dad will be really happy with this barrow, he can use it in the garden and save all our backs."

"What are we goin to use the bricks for?" Norrice asked.

"Don't know, Dad will think of something," Desmond answered.

The boys arrived home tired and hungry after a long day, but their excitement regarding the wheelbarrow overwhelmed everything else. The other boys came out to look, followed by Ike. "What's this?" Ike said.

"It's for you, Dad. We got it for ya from a building site, they had two of um," Desmond said excitedly.

"So you stole it then?" Ike was calm.

"Sort of, but they had two of um dad, they wunna miss it," Norrice added.

"What have I told you about taking things that don't

belong to you?" Ike was starting to get a little louder. "Take it back to where you got it from NOW! It's not yours." Ike was adamant and with the look in his eyes the boys knew better than to argue.

"Okay, Dad, we can do it tomorrow," Norrice said disappointed.

"Tomorrow!" Ike said. "You will take it back now, no argument." Ike insisted.

Desmond opened his mouth to speak, "NOW!" repeated Ike.

Looking at each other the two boys knew they had no choice. Grabbing their hats, they turned the wheelbarrow around and started the long walk back to the building site.

About half an hour into the long walk, Desmond said, "Hey, brother we are not taking all these bricks back, it's too heavy. See them trees, we can tip 'em there, no one will know." It didn't take much for Norrice to agree.

"Why don't we just tip the barrow up and leave the lots?" Norrice suggested. "Not a bad idea, our kid, but we will have to sit around for an hour or dad will know we didn't go all the way back," Desmond said.

Norrice agreed again. "Good idea, I wunna say a word."

"Do you think you were a bit hard on the lads, Ike?" Sally asked.

"Maybe, but they won't do it again will they?" He replied with a small grin on his face.

CHAPTER EIGHT
Scrumping

Sally noticed young Norman was becoming very quiet, especially over the last couple of weeks, which was not at all like him. He was normally the loudest of her children, and a nuisance according to his brothers. Herbert had accused him of being a pain in the arse on many occasions.

She had become aware he was going to school, eating, and sleeping and that's all. His face always looked like a week of wet Sundays.

She told Ike her observation, explaining that she was worried. He was not talking to anyone, not going out to play with his friends. In fact, if he did go outside, he just sat on the cold stone step, the same cold step Ike had sat on when each of the children had been born

When she had asked Norman if he was all right, or if he felt ill, he just shrugged his shoulders or mumbled his stock answer, "I'm right, Ma."

Sally thought it must be the growing pains of an eight-year-old boy, but she had never noticed this with the other boys. She decided to keep a closer eye on him.

Saturday morning, Desmond and Norrice had taken Toby and gone off hunting. Derrek was helping Ike with the pigs and chickens. Herbert had run down to help his Granddad Zac with his chickens, and Joyce was cooking with Sally.

Norman once again sat quietly on the back stone step, deep in thought, picking up bits of wood and stones and tossing them haphazardly into the garden.

His short pants did nothing to protect him from the coldness of the stone step, but he didn't notice.

Suddenly he stood straight, looked around and pulled a sack from the top of the coal shed, and wondered out into the street.

Looking both ways, as if deciding which way to go, he finally turned to the right, stopping at a wooden gate a few houses up from his own. Opening the gate, he walked down the side of the house, and into the huge back yard.

The man who owned the property was Mr Eric Woodward, a stout man with a large beard and a thunderous voice. He had never married, and was used to his own company, and didn't suffer children easily

There were ten massive apple trees, in Mr Woodward's orchard. And to a little boy's eyes it was the biggest orchard in the world.

No one knew what he did with all the apples, although many were left to rot on the ground.

Norman had decided he was going scrumping for some of the apples. He had never done this before, but how hard could it be to climb a tree and drop apples into a sack.

He picked a fully laden tree, and slowly climbed to the middle fork, rested his sac on the branch, he started to pull the shiny green apples from their hanging place, and drop them into the sack. *This is easy*, he thought, *I should have done this weeks ago.*

Norman could almost smell the lovely apple pies his mother would make.

Looking up, through the branches, he saw the biggest apple he had ever seen, he had to get that apple, it was big enough to make a pie all by itself. The lovely big green apple had to be his.

But, when he leaned across to grab the branch above his head, his footing slipped, Norman came tumbling from the tree.

"Ouch!" he cried out in pain.

He pulled himself to a sitting position, leaning against the tree, supporting his right wrist in his left hand, he started to cry. He could not move his wrist without pain searing up his arm. He had also scraped his knees and they were both bleeding. He was injured, but he couldn't go home, his dad would be angry he had been scrumping. He needed time to stop his wrist hurting.

Looking around, he saw a little brown shed near the last tree, with the door ajar. He pulled himself to his feet, and, limping, he headed for the shed.

Inside there were tools, and boxes full of apples, some starting to rot. The smell was very strong. He could hear someone whistling outside, it was getting louder, and coming close to the shed. *Maybe Mr Woodward would shoot me for stealing apples*, he thought, so he lay down quickly and hid behind the boxes.

Mr Woodward entered and placed his spade and gardening fork behind the door of the shed. He did not notice Norman. Stepping out of the shed, he closed the door, and locked it. Then he continued to whistle as he walked back toward his house.

It was dark in the shed, no windows had been added when building it. Norman hated the dark, he was getting scared now.

He could hear all the creeks of the wood, the movement of the trees. His mind started imagining what might be sharing the shed with him. "What if there is a rat, or a spider I can't see," he said to himself. "Or what about snakes." He hated even the thought of a snake. Even though he had never seen a snake, his imagination was running wild. He curled into as small a ball as he could sobbing quietly and waited, hoping to be found.

Sally called out to everyone that dinner was ready, a hearty chicken stew and dumpling. When Norman didn't join them, she asked the other kids where he was, as they came through the door. No one had seen him since the morning.

It was dark outside now. Ike told the boys to get their coats, and go with him to look for Norman. "Sally, keep dinner warm, we won't be long." Norrice and Herbert took Toby and ran across the fields calling out his name. Ike and Derek walked one way down the street calling out. Desmond ran the opposite way.

Ike heard something. "Be quiet!" he shouted, holding up his hands, and turning his head from side to side. "Can you hear that?"

"No," Derek said. "What can you hear?"

"Shh!" Keeping his hands raised, he started to walk closer to Mr Woodward's gate. Then he stopped again, listened, and called out Norman's name.

"Dad! Dad! I'm here in the shed," reaching the shed, Ike tried the door but it was locked.

"I will be back, I am getting Mr Woodward to unlock the door."

Ike banged on Mr Woodward's front door.

"What's going on?" Mr Woodward said as he opened the door.

"Evening Eric, I think Norman has got himself locked in your shed," Ike said.

Mr Woodward grabbed his keys, and Ike and Derrek followed him through the orchard, to the shed.

"What's he doing in my bloody shed?" he said.

Ike could hear Norman crying from inside as Mr Woodward unlocked the door. Norman called out, "I hurt me arm, Dad."

Mr Woodward was not happy Norman had been on his property, and less happy with the sack of apples at the foot of the tree, "Do you condone stealing, Mr Murby?"

"Not at all, Mr Woodard, rest assured Norman will pay for the apples he picked."

Ike carried him out of the shed, and after thanking and apologising to Mr Woodward again, carried him home.

Sally and the other kids were relieved to see him, but Sally's worry soon turned to anger. She scolded him for being gone so long, and not telling anyone where he was going.

Ike bandaged Norman's swollen and sore wrist and put it in a sling.

"Just a sprain, lad," he said, as he started to clean his bloodied knees.

"I have belly ache, Mam" Norman said, feeling sorry for himself.

"You are probably hungry, me lad" Sally said, offering a bowl of the chicken stew.

"No, I ain't hungry, I ate four apples. Just a bad pain in me belly"

"Four of those sour apples? No wonder you have belly ache."

"Anyway, why were you in old man Woodward's

Orchard?" Desmond asked.

"I wanted to help, like all of you, a job to bring summut for the table."

Sally let out a long sigh, "Stealing apples from Mr Woodward is not helping, I'm sure Mr Woodward will find you work on Saturday to pay for them."

"Well how many did ya get?" Desmond asked

"None! Them apples is horrible, and sour, no good for a pie." Norman said pulling a face.

Everyone burst out laughing, as Norman was given a dose of Epsom salts and sent off to bed.

CHAPTER NINE
A Family Grown

Friday night was Sally and Ike's regular night out. They would pop off for a few drinks up the road to 'The Man Within the Compass' or 'The Rag and Mop' as it had become known. Sally always enjoyed a few Guinness's and everyone who came into the pub would buy her a drink.

George Waite entered, spotting Sally.

"Evening, Sally. Can I get you a Guinness?"

"Ah thank ya, George," Sally said.

"Where's Ike tonight?" George asked.

"He's round back having a smoke and chin wag," Sally said.

Just then Sammy Worthington came in, "Ay up Sally love, can I get ya one in?" Before Sally could answer, George turned to Sammy and said, "I'm already getting her one."

Sammy replied, "No ya not, I jus said I'll get er one."

As they both stood at the bar arguing about who was buying the Guinness, Sally got up and walked over to the bar, put her arms around both men's shoulders and said, "Stop ya bloody arguing, I'll 'ave one from each of ya." They laughed, and Sally ended up with two drinks in. At closing time she and Ike walked home singing as usual.

A lovely Saturday morning, the sun came through the window. It was a bit chilly outside, but the sun shine made it feel like Summer.

Joyce seemed to have a skip in her step this morning, and was certainly getting through her chores quicker than normal. Was it the sight of the sun, or was there something else on her mind?

"I am going out tonight, Mam," Joyce informed her mother.

"Somewhere nice by the look on your face," Sally replied.

"I am going to the dance hall, that's all, with Wilf. I met him last Saturday at the dance," Joyce said with a faraway look in her eyes.

"What's his last name?" Sally asked.

"Berridge," Joyce replied, "Don't think you would know the family ma, he lives in Shepshed."

"Make sure you're home before eleven, or ya dad will not let you go again." Ike was stricter on Joyce than any of the boys, Sally thought this unfair but most fathers were harder on the girls.

Six months earlier, Joyce had complained about the boys getting away with murder, saying it's not fair. After her complaining had ceased, Ike asked her if she was finished. Then he got close to her, and looking right into her eyes he said

"Ya think ya hard done to then, do you? Well how about this, you're not going anywhere today young lady. While you're under my roof, you will do as I say." After that Joyce learnt to take what she could get, and not to complain.

Sally gave Ike a stern look at the time, and Ike knew what she was thinking.

"You have to be stricter with ya girls to protect um from boys," Ike argued.

"What about our boys. There're out and about with

someone's daughter. I just don't see the difference." But Ike was not having any of it.

"Me decision is made, let that be the end of it." Ike was adamant.

Ironing her best dress, a floral, below-knee length with a waisted belt, a small half collar, and a princess neckline, with matching headband.

Joyce proceeded to wash and curl her hair and sat in the sun to dry it a little quicker. She was to meet Wilf at the front door of the dance hall at seven.

Wilfred Lenard Berridge was a happy type of chap, always with a smile on his face. He was tall, and slim with brown short well-groomed hair. He was two years older than Joyce, and just six months out of his army conscription, although he remained on the reserve list for another four years. He was working in the agriculture department of the Whitwick quarry.

He felt like the luckiest man alive that Joyce had agreed to see him again. The feelings were mutual, Joyce thought Wilf very good looking, a good catch.

As she was leaving home, around six p.m., Ike called out, "Joyce, make sure he walks you ALL the way home, or he will have me to answer to."

Joyce raised her eyes to the sky and replied, "Yes, Dad."

"No good raising your eyes up to heaven, he won't help you if Wilf doesn't walk you home." Sally said.

Joyce and Wilf started courting seriously, and after a year or so, and with their parents blessing, they became engaged just before Christmas, 1950.

Desmond and Norrice had gone out early, before even Ike was out of bed.

Running across the fields, where they usually hunted rabbits, but today was different. Today Norrice had told Desmond he needed his assistance with something important. Desmond was so intrigued, he had gone along without question. Norrice grabbed his dad's axe from the coal shed.

"Come on, our kid, get a riddle on, before everyone gets up," Norrice said.

After about half an hour walking Norrice stopped, looked at Desmond and said, "Look at that pine tree, ain't it the best Christmas tree you ever saw?"

Desmond had to agree, it was a perfect triangle shaped pine tree, dark green, about six feet tall standing all alone in a field, with no other pine trees to be seen. Norrice was sure they were destined to have this tree for Christmas.

They had only ever had a tiny Christmas tree for as long as he could remember. Now all the kids were older, a larger tree was called for.

This year would be different, they would have a tree to be proud of.

Pulling his father's axe from his belt, Norrice proceeded to chop down the tree. "Hold it steady, Desmond, I don't want to spoil the shape," he said.

They lifted the felled tree over their shoulders, and together carried it home.

Before they had left home, Norrice had told Herbert to have a bucket of dirt ready for their return, which Herbert had dutifully done. When they put the trunk right down in the bucket of dirt the tree looked magnificent.

Sally liked it as well and agreed they had gone long enough without a proper Christmas tree.

"This tree is so big there will be no room for the family,"

Sarah laughed.

Norman and Joyce set about cutting paper shapes and paper lanterns to decorate it. Derek made a large cardboard star, which he painted white for the top of the tree. When Ike came home, he commented how nice and festive the house looked, and more than that, how well they had all worked together to make this Christmas the best so far.

Christmas was enjoyed by everyone. Wilf was invited to share Christmas dinner, and Ike had managed to get a beautiful big turkey which Sally slow roasted with stuffing, and potatoes, and knobs that had gone through a frost, and the runner beans she had salted during Summer. They finished with homemade Christmas plum pudding with lashings of custard. The family had a lot to be grateful for that year.

After dinner, Joyce helped Sally clean up, before she headed off to Wilf's family for tea. Derek and Norman were playing snap with a pack of playing cards.

Desmond and Ike were having a smoke outside and discussing the lovely Christmas they'd had. Norrice and Herbert were both fast asleep in the armchairs of the best room.

"Well now, I think 1951 is going to be a great year." Sally said, and Ike had to agree.

February 1951, twenty-three-year-old Desmond and his brothers, Herbert and Norrice,, met up with a couple of buddies, and decided to try the dance hall again looking for girls. The Murby boys were on the prowl.

They were all good dancers, having being taught at school the waltz, foxtrot and quickstep.

The boys had taught each other how to boogie woogie and bunny hop.

Swing was really popular at the dance halls, and all the girls wanted to dance all night. It was on this night Desmond met Winnie Manders, the two danced all night drinking and laughing. Desmond really liked her and Winnie definitely thought he was dapper. He walked her home to St Bernard's Road, they then made arrangements to meet again the following week. After a few goodnight kisses, Winnifred's Dad banged on the window, she knew it was time to go in.

Winnie was the eldest of five children, she was born January 21st, 1930. Her sister, Pat was two years younger, then came her brother, Roy, followed by another sister, Joan, and finally her brother, Maurice; their parents were Wilfred and Gwendoline Manders.

She was actually christened Gwendoline Winnifred Louisa, after both her parents, but was known as Winnie. She was a striking girl with wavy brown hair, about five and half feet tall. She worked at the dumps hosiery factory, being trained on the sewing machines. The factory was about half an hour walk each day from her house.

Until recently she had been engaged to be married, but she and Rubin had broken off their engagement. After talking about it at length, they both felt they acted hastily and made the mutual decision to break up.

Winnie really liked Desmond, and he seemed to like her. The couple continued to meet regularly, going to the Connie club, the dance hall, and walks across the forest, all the common outings for courting couples.

May, 1951, Wilf and Joyce were married two months after she turned twenty-four, in a small ceremony with just family and close friends, at St John the Baptist church in Whitwick, starting their married life in Shepshed, going on to have five children. Janet, Graham, Maureen, Marie and Gary.

It was around the same time that Winnie informed Desmond she was to have his child. Desmond needed to think about this, he was only twenty-three and Winnie only twenty-one. He loved Winnie, but, marriage and family was a huge step, and a great responsibility. After a couple days Desmond talked things over with his father, while they were feeding the canaries, and sharing a cigarette.

Ike listened intently, as Desmond spoke of the child Winnie was carrying, of his hopes for the future and marriage. Then Ike turned to face Desmond and said with a lot of sincerity, "Desmond, Winnie is a nice young woman who clearly loves you. If she is good enough for sex, then she is good enough to marry. You need to do the right thing and go to see the vicar."

On August 18th, 1951, Desmond, the second of Ike and Sally's children, was married to Winnie. At the same church, where only three months earlier, Joyce had married Wilf.

Although Winnie had four siblings living at home, there was more room at her parents' two storey council home, with three bedrooms, a large combined living and dining room, plus a big kitchen, and a washhouse they did not have to share with other families. Desmond and Winnie would live in the spare downstairs room and share the bathroom and kitchen with the rest of the family.

Winnie had picked names for a girl and a boy, well before the baby was due. She was convinced she was carrying a girl and chose the name Sandra Elizabeth, for a boy it would be Michael Desmond.

March 24th, 1952, Winnie gave birth to their first child, a girl, but they had changed their mind on the name for the child,

Sandra Elizabeth, becoming Christine Ann.

'Christine Ann Murby' suited her better. She was doted on and loved by her parents and grandparents.

One month later, in the same church that her parents were married, Christine was christened.

Desmond and Winnie had a second child, this time a boy, and named him Michael Desmond, born June 8th, 1956. By this time, they had moved into their own council house on the Greenhill estate. And their family was now complete.

March 1955 saw Norrice marry the love of his life, Joan Shaw, and they had a son, Steven.

March 1956, Herbert married Hilda Lowe at Whitwick church, and together had a son, Richard. Herbert became stepfather to Keith and Peter Lowe. Whose brave father had been a soldier, and passed away when they were younger.

March 1958, Derek married his fiancée Joan Sibson, at the same Whitwick church. They had three children; Valerie, Andrew, and Alison.

April 1963 Norman married his Scottish girlfriend, Christine Scanlon in Grenock, Scotland. They had three children; Vincent, Karen, and Christopher.

Sally and Ike were now the proud grandparents, and had fifteen grandchildren, and two step-grandchildren. They could not have been happier.

There was plenty of room now in their little two up, two down house. Ike only had his canaries to look after. Everything was quiet, and easy… Until the grandchildren descended for a visit, which was often.

Ike and Sally Murby centre their children L _ R Joyce, Herbert, Derek, Norrice, Norman and Desmond.

Desmond and Winifred's wedding 1951 both Murby and Manders families.

Sally and Ike 1970

Sarah Parker circa 1920 - 1930

Monastery Mount St Bernard's Abby photo by CJ

Coalville clock tower 2015 photo CJ

Medal for war exemption due to reserved occupation.

Gunn hill house Photo kindly permitted by Tom Clayton

Man Within the Compass circa 1990- 2006 CJ

Man Within the Compass circa 1990- 2006 CJ